Because divorce has invad[...]
this book should be a great help t[...]
I believe each one reading this boc[...] [...] a lot of good,
practical advice.

Ruth Bell Graham
Author, *Prodigals and Those Who Love Them*

Marjorie understands broken families like no one else I know. Her book gives hope to older parents who see their children's marriages disintegrate.

Archibald Hart
Professor of Psychology, Fuller Theological Seminary

This book could be [God's] instrument to help bring healing to any family's relationships shattered by divorce.

Vonette Bright
Director, Women Today International

Marjorie Lee Chandler covers it all in *After Your Child Divorces*. Believe that for every problem God will provide a solution ... God uses life's bruises.

Robert Schuller
Founding Pastor, Crystal Cathedral Ministries

... A splendid gift to parents whose minds are boggled and hearts are broken when a child whose happiness they prayed for is sadly divorced.

Lewis Smedes
Author, *Shame and Grace*

... In clear, right-to-the-point style, Marjorie Lee Chandler has provided real help for families suddenly immersed in the flood of feelings and real-life problems unleashed by divorce. No quick fixes, but practical insights undergirded by love.

Lewis and Melissa McBurney
Founders and Therapists, Marble Retreat

Certainly this book is "scratching where there's an itch." We honor Marjorie for this [book]. . . .

Ray and Anne Ortlund
Founders, Renewal Ministries

At last ... a book that moves beyond the pain of the past and helps us reach for the promise of new beginnings. Essential reading for anyone who has been through the anguish of divorce.

Fay Angus
Author and Speaker

Every parent ... will find help and hope in this compassionate book. It is poignant, timely, practical and honest. Each chapter is a blueprint for rebuilding family bonds—even during the relational aftershocks.

Les and Leslie Parrott
Authors, *Saving Your Marriage Before It Starts*

With tenderness, insight, and wisdom, Marjorie Lee Chandler gives needed direction and advice. . . . From the initial pain through the turbulent times of transition, this book guides a parent to a place of rebuilding and reconciliation.

Betty Southard
Coauthor, *The Grandparenting Book*

In this book . . . midlife parents move through pain to being redemptive agents. You will read it more than once.

Gary Chapman
Pastor and Author, *The Five Love Languages*

I welcome this honest and straightforward depiction of divorce and its awful consequences, but I cheer even more loudly for its offer of hope and healing.

William E. Pannell
Dean of the Chapel, Fuller Theological Seminary

I wish Jan and I had had this book when one of our children divorced. Marjorie Lee Chandler has drawn not only a realistic picture of what to expect when one of your children divorces, but gives hope and help in how to rebuild your family and hold on to the relationships you treasure. The journaling and discussion sections are priceless!

David Stoop, Ph.D.
Psychologist and Author, *Experiencing God Together*

This book fills a real need, given the fact that six in ten new marriages will break up through divorce or separation. . . . With compassion and biblical insight this author offers hope, comfort, and practical advice to the many Americans who suffer silently in the always painful aftermath of divorce.

George Gallup Jr.
Chairman, The George H. Gallup International Institute

There are many refined, specially tooled instruments of healing needed in today's broken world. Marjorie Lee Chandler has provided us with one that will most certainly offer help and hope to those whose families have experienced the splintering force of a divorce-quake.

Jack W. Hayford, D. Litt.
Senior Pastor, The Church On The Way

After Your Child Divorces is must reading for every mother and father who has ached through the divorce of a son or daughter. It is insightful, practical, loving, and healing in its honest message of hope and rebuilding after the tragedy of divorce strikes the heart of your home.

Jim Smoke
Author, *Growing Through Divorce*

Rebuilding Family Bonds...

After Your Child Divorces

Marjorie Lee Chandler

Foreword by
Louis and Colleen Evans

ZondervanPublishingHouse
Grand Rapids, Michigan

A Division of HarperCollinsPublishers

After Your Child Divorces
Copyright © 1997 by Marjorie Lee Chandler

Requests for information should be addressed to:

ZondervanPublishingHouse
Grand Rapids, Michigan 49530

Library of Congress Cataloging-in-Publication Data

Chandler, Marjorie Lee, 1935–
    After your child divorces / Marjorie Lee Chandler
    p.   cm.
    ISBN: 0-310-20554-9 (softcover)
    1. Parent and adult child. 2. Divorced people—Family relationships. 3.
Divorce—Psychological aspects. 4. Divorce—Religious aspects—Christianity. I.
Title.
HQ814.C43 1997
306.89—dc20   96-35832
                                                     CIP

Grateful acknowledgment is made to Mercy Publishing for permission to reprint a
portion of *Spirit Song* by John Wimber, Mercy/Vineyard Publishing 1979.

Names and some minor facts in the stories in this book have been changed to
maintain confidentiality.

The author has made every effort to make the information and suggestions in this
book practical and workable, but neither she nor the publisher assumes any
responsibility for successes, failures, or other results of putting these ideas into
practice.

Printed in the United States of America

96 97 98 99 00 01 02 03 /❖ DH/ 10 9 8 7 6 5 4 3 2 1

For more information regarding speaking opportunities on family-related topics for women or couples, please write to:

Marjorie Lee Chandler
c/o Creative Communications
1988 Old Mission Drive B–1 Room 206
Solvang, CA 93460

You may also e-mail: ChandlerML@aol.com

After Your Child Divorces *is dedicated
to four mid-generation parents:
Jerry and Janet Barton and
Louis and Mary Jo Ortega,
exemplary survivors of the divorce
of an adult child in their respective families.
Both of these Christian couples have
demonstrated a parenting style
that looks back in peace and ahead in hope.
I am honored to count them, and their
adult children, among my closest friends.
Their wonderful extended families
have inspired me.*

CONTENTS

Foreword. 9
Introduction: Picking Up the Pieces 11

Part 1
AFTER YOUR CHILD DIVORCES

1. Hearing the News—and Surviving! 17
2. Growing Through the Pain 32
3. Listening to Your Divorced Son or Daughter 46
4. Staying in Touch with Your Single-Again Child 61
5. Coping with Singles Back Home Again 75
6. Dealing with Sex, Substance Abuse, and Money 87

Part 2
REBUILDING FAMILY BONDS

7. Adapting to New Family Circles 103
8. Encouraging the Healing Process. 116
9. Managing Anger and Building Trust 129
10. Polishing the Friendship Between Parent
    and Adult Child 140
11. Linking the Family Through Grandparenting 154
12. Relating to Grandchildren of Divorce 170
13. Bonding Through Friendship, Love, and Hope 184
Resources 197
Notes. 201

FOREWORD

In one of Colleen's earliest childhood memories, she is about four or five. She and her single-parent mother had just moved from the warm womb of Colleen's grandfather's house, where they had taken refuge after her mother's divorce. They had barely unloaded the old Chevy when the neighborhood children gathered to welcome the new kid on the block. Forming a circle, they begin to skip and sing: "Ring-Around-the-Rosey; Colleen doesn't have a daddy!" That day, for the first time, she became conscious of divorce and the pain that keeps it company.

Nowadays, the hole in our family ozone layer has grown, allowing the harmful rays of rupture and rejection to affect our culture in destructive ways. Divorce seems almost epidemic: Where is the family that has not in some way experienced the anguish of broken relationships that end in divorce?

When we were the senior pastor family of La Jolla (California) Presbyterian Church in the 1960s and '70s, we met an attractive, bright young mother. Her children and ours played together with the happy chortles of childhood. But soon we saw in Marjorie the signs of deep and painful struggle. Not long after, her dysfunctional marriage came unglued at great cost.

During those years of ministry, we saw many people face the excruciating pain of divorce. We heard the wails of agony erupting from the soul of a divorcing man. We walked the trail of loneliness with single mothers. We saw feelings of anger from children of divorce. Amidst all the pain, we also saw the grace of Jesus Christ give resilience and hope to foundering lives.

This was Marjorie's own story: ML, as she is now called, used the cinders of a tragic experience to make new building blocks. She kept other family relationships productive and allowed our Lord to change tragedy into triumph. For the past eighteen years she has been blessed with a beautiful second marriage to Russell Chandler.

"Living to the praise of God's glory" is the dynamic that transformed ML's life; it can also transform you and your children going through the pain of divorce. Parents are not exempt from the pain. We know. We, too, have experienced that valley with one of our four children.

When their children are young, parents find it easier to trust them to Christ; when they are grown, we cannot so easily "fix things." But there is real spiritual beauty in watching an adult child find a new life with God's leading—a unique and stunning art form made only out of recycled pain.

As parents, our tearful eyes can behold a once-suffering child become a giant in faith. Persevering through personal pain, our divorced sons and daughters "grow up" in spirit. We are amazed at their sensitivity and ability to help others. The path of grace has matured them beyond our dreams!

Now our longtime friend ML has written helpfully and hopefully about recovery from divorce. Her research is thorough, and she offers many creative, practical ways that we as parents and extended family can support our wounded members. "Divorce ends marriage, not a family," writes ML.

We are avid family advocates, so we quite naturally resonate with and value ML's emphasis on building and maintaining strong family ties. We believe that this "vessel of family" is one of the ways God maintains a witness to himself. His unconditional love is the essential tie that binds all families together.

In the pages that follow, ML invites you, the parents, to walk this path of grace as your divorced child learns to trust again. It is a book filled with hope and healing. We commend our friend for writing it, and we heartily commend it to you.

Colleen and Louis H. Evans
Renewal Ministries
Bass Lake, California

INTRODUCTION

PICKING UP THE PIECES

With serious concentration, our four-year-old granddaughter Sarah lined up a legion of dominoes across our broad kitchen windowsill. Carefully, gingerly, she positioned each white-dotted piece. "Stand tall!" Sarah seemed to command.

Then . . . *ping, ping, ping!* the slender slices flattened with a *rat-a-tat-tat*. Startled, Sarah watched the meandering row collapse in a flash. What had she done? Her expressive black eyes caught mine, revealing momentary, unexpected confusion.

Later I thought of how, as a teenager, I had lined up my "life dominoes": a job right out of high school, a scholarship for four years of college, a professional position. As a young speech and language therapist I was fulfilled in many ways. But the domino of marriage was not yet in place.

As true with most women of the late '50s, marriage was an important piece in my life journey. It would stabilize my future, I thought. It would be a fairy-tale relationship withstanding whatever made other marriages topple.

My eighteen-year marriage stacked out like a long line of dominoes—two new homes, three children, career advances for my spouse. Although the marriage line was wobbly from the beginning, divorce was not an option. At least not for me. I wouldn't. I couldn't!

Like Sarah, I don't quite know which weakness precipitated the collapse. I know my health broke, and so did my marriage. In 1970 I spent long summer months in the hospital

11

hanging onto a thin thread of hope. Major intestinal surgery saved my life, but I came home to a "singles" bed. I was angry! *At life? At God?* I wasn't clear *at what*, but I knew the turmoil. I was alone, with outdated professional credentials, frustrated and discouraged. Didn't anyone care?

Surely my parents would understand my pain. My mother came to visit just a few months before the separation. Didn't she see the strain on my face, the hurt in my heart? No. She saw only a daughter gone astray of her own romanticized ideal. A this-is-not-the-way-you-were-supposed-to-turn-out daughter.

Never mind that both our pastor and a psychiatrist had said the marriage was unworkable after attempts at joint counseling. Never mind that I had elected to continue long-term counseling alone, trusting against all odds for a miracle. My mother was adamant and unyielding. She spoke only of *how-could-you-do-this-to-me!*

I kept my ache inside.

My father and stepmother lived several states away. I visited them that fateful summer, hoping to have my wounded spirits soothed. Wrong again. Although my father had once himself been divorced, he offered little compassion. *My plight is only causing him to relive his own oft-broken life*, I rationalized. My stepmother lectured me about the sin of divorce. No, it was more demeaning than that: I heard that *I* was sinful—the evil of divorce was let off the hook more easily than I was.

I believe that divorce is wrong. Even stronger, I believe that divorce is a sinful situation. But sins, whatever they are, are forgivable. That's what God's grace is all about. His forgiveness frees us to go on with life.

As William Barclay wrote, "We must believe, not only that God exists, but also that God cares." I wrote this book because God cares and wants to be involved in every domino of our fragile journey here on earth.

Sometimes couples can't hold back the tumbles; transgressions in life are a minuscule reflection of the original fall in Eden. Parents can unwittingly withhold God's love from their hurting adult children after the fall of divorce. May these chapters guide you in rebuilding your family circle and filling it with hope.

Part 1

AFTER YOUR CHILD DIVORCES

1

HEARING THE NEWS— AND SURVIVING!

"Mom, John and I are getting a divorce." No matter how quietly they're spoken, these words slam against your heart and leave you breathless. Yet divorce happens, and in the best of families.

Like an unforeseen tornado, a child's divorce often comes upon a parent with little warning.[1] "Why didn't we know?" cries an angry, middle-aged father. "We're too old" ..."too busy" ... "too tired." "Why us? Why now?" "For weeks," murmurs a distraught mother upon the news of her son's divorce announcement, "I felt like a fragile dandelion seed swirling in a gale." And the windstorm strikes everyone, causing pain to zigzag through the lives of your divorced son or daughter, your grandchildren—and you.

Life is askew. You feel assaulted. Stress keeps you awake. You can't think straight, food is tasteless, and your prayers seem shallow. Hopefully, someone will explain that you're experiencing normal grief—the initial feelings from significant loss.

In a broken nest there are no whole eggs. "Make no mistake about it, divorce inflicts terrible pain on its victims," says psychologist Dr. James Dobson of Focus on the Family. "Every member of the family suffers when a marriage blows up."[2] With the uprooting of divorce, a family tree is split and all the branches shake.

As we hiked together one day, my friend Nan expressed fears common to parents of married children. Halfway down from our 2,500-foot-elevation climb to the snow line in the dead of winter, Nan and I were glad for a grassy spot to stop for lunch. We took off our perspiration-dampened socks, unzipped our backpacks, and enjoyed a breathtaking view of the Santa Ynez Valley below. As we munched hard-boiled eggs and trail mix, we wiggled our toes in the winter sun and talked about things most middle-aged moms talk about—our adult children and grandchildren.

Nan and her husband enjoy close-by grandparenting—one son and family next door, another son and family just a few miles away. Although none of Nan's grown children are divorced, she mused about her impression of the disruptions divorce causes.

"If one of my sons got divorced it would really crush me," Nan said, thoughtfully. "The ex-spouse would probably remarry, and then my grandchildren would have a new stepfather and other grandparents—maybe even live far away. If divorce hit one of our families it would forever change my relationship with my kids."

Like so many parents who fear one day waking up to divorce in the family, Nan knew it would mean stretching her circle of love. Someone has said, "Divorce is a death that never dies." When we lose a family member by natural death, we mourn, but we know we did not cause the demise. After divorce, however, parents painfully ponder how they might have prevented the calamity.

BLAME

A parent's first reaction upon receiving the news is to find someone to blame. "When my son's marriage fell apart I felt I'd somehow failed as a parent," laments Nancy, who says she wore a "happy face" to mask her hurt.

"My mind churned with 'if onlys,'" says Barbara, another overwhelmed mother. Barbara is not sympathetic with her son's decision to divorce: "My son was absolutely in the wrong. . . . I'll never forget the hopelessness I felt when only weeks later he showed up with a new partner. Seeing them hand in hand made me want to throw up!" Other parents talked about being "numb and in a state of shock" or spoke about "the crazies."

Lynette's dad is possessive of "his baby," the only daughter. He is angry and revengeful toward his former son-in-law. And Kevin's dad aches for his divorced son, whom he feels has been "kicked down low." Harold talks about mixed feelings toward his divorced daughter, Abbie, who calls him nearly every day. "She depends on me like a husband," he explains. "It boosts my ego, but it's also binding."

Divorce isn't a single ingredient; it's a stew pot of various problems. Foul parts of personalities, long shrouded from sight, are now seen as they bubble to the top. Your adult child may be faced with troubles you never dreamed she would have—physical abuse, drugs, homosexuality, infidelity, and other irresponsible behaviors.

Parents—even the best of parents—can neither force their grown children to do what is best for them nor prevent them from doing things that are harmful to themselves and others. Some parents face humiliation, tension, sorrow, or at least social embarrassment, because of their adult children's choices. Parents need to learn how to handle the unpleasant and unpredictable, how to cope without placing blame.

Mark, in his fifties, seemed to shrink down in guilt after his son's divorce, wondering if he'd been too selfish, unloving, or aloof. Phil, another dejected dad of two divorced sons, thinks he was "too easy on them growing up." "Maybe too hard," muses another. Fathers take on guilt from both extremes. They feel as if they should have *done something;* but those who try to intervene in their son's or daughter's marriage often feel frustrated when their "solutions" don't work. Taking on unnecessary guilt keeps parents from constructive involvement. God calls us to be human beings—not human doings.

Your divorcing adult child is not a failure, though he may be involved in *circumstances* of failure. But your child's divorce can be a turning point for you. The Chinese phrase "I Ching" defines the meaning of "crisis" as "dangerous opportunity." Because of your child's divorce, you have been unwittingly tossed into an opportunity for personal growth.

SHAME

For families with fundamental beliefs, divorce is still shocking. Accepting divorce is more difficult for Christians because of the idealized perception that bad things don't happen to good people. One mother says, "I felt rejected by God. I stayed in bed a lot; I was so depressed that my husband was truly frightened." Another: "I thought if you raised your children in the church this wouldn't happen."

Denial weaves in and out of the saga of parents who cannot face severe discord and divorce in their family. They say with rancor, "In my day, we stuck it out!" For several years, Henry and Trish Hough, with two divorced daughters living in other cities, told none of their friends their dark secret. Fearing embarrassment and judgment, they carried their shame inside.

Say the authors of *Family Secrets:*

> Secret-keeping families are based on guilt and shame....
> For families living with secrets, the loneliness can be terribly isolating, especially if they consider their secrets disgraceful.... They are isolated by the fear that the truth would destroy them.[3]

Encouraged by the warmth of a church covenant group, the Houghs finally revealed the secret of divorce in their family. When they did, they found sympathy, not condemnation. Truth and freedom usually go together (see John 8:32).

Name your sorrows, whatever they are. Don't hide them in an inner sanctum of shame. Confessing with one another liberates us from loads too heavy to carry.

PAIN

I've heard too many real-life stories not to believe that parents hurt from divorce in their families. And knowing that an avalanche of divorces has rolled over this country in the past two decades doesn't ease a parent's pain. Each divorce carries its own mark of tragedy within the family circle. Most midlife parents agree with the Yiddish proverb: "Small children disturb your sleep, big children your life."

Divorce is a snap of the branch of relationship, and each severed relationship is a little death. "When a marriage relationship breaks and breaks for good, we die a death right there.... And the rest of the self feels pain for the loss,"[4] says Walter Wangerin in *Mourning into Dancing*. Divorce is like a stinger that can't be easily pulled out—at least, not without it hurting.

Just as no healthy person chooses pain, no parent chooses the pain of divorce for his or her child—it just comes. Take heart, the Bible is filled with men and women whose faith was fashioned in pain. It is the low points in life that teach us most about trusting God.

Etched forever in Heddy's memory is the day her son, Ron, looking bedraggled and defeated, stood on their doorstep. "It's all over, Mom," he said simply.

Over? What's over? "I couldn't imagine!" Heddy says, recalling her initial thoughts. *Had he lost his shirt on a red-hot stock? His job? Maybe just a gamble on a ball game . . . Surely not his marriage.*

"Yes, Mom—she wants out. Will you take me in?"

"In all my years as a mother," Heddy says, "I can think of no time more difficult. It was as if lightning had split the sky in two.

"In the months that followed, I watched our professionally capable son struggle through crushing personal pain—division of property, custody battles, wrenching weekends of less-than-happy visitation, and loss of effectiveness in his work. Ron's stress spiraled into physical pain—headaches, sleepless nights, and warning signs of ulcers.

"During this ordeal, Lloyd and I had our own pain," adds Heddy, a straitlaced lady who had grown up in an era when the word "divorce" was barely whispered. "We felt so alone—caught in a web we didn't spin. A web that also kept our son prey. We lay awake and wondered what to do. The night held no answers, and the days brought new pain as the grandchildren seemed to shun us."

Like Heddy, many parents say that by the time they learned about the marital breakup, the decision could not be reversed. Instead, they had to deal with the reality of divorce. My friend, writer Dolly Patterson, talks about emotional healing: "The most effective way to begin to redeem failure is to examine the tapestry of our spiritual life and to resolve, with God's help, to mend what is torn and broken there." Patterson says that even though failure is wrapped in a blanket of pain, "it can protect us from further harm and redirect us toward achieving our goals and dreams."[5]

In time, the wounds created by divorce in the family may heal. In the meantime, pain is real. We may keep it out of sight and out of mind, but pushed down, pain festers and seeps into unexpected veins in our lives. As we will see later on, it's okay to cry out to God in our pain, our fear, and our frustration. In his book *When God Doesn't Make Sense*, James Dobson says to "lean into pain . . . God will use the difficulty for His purposes—and, indeed, for our own good."[6] To clean-sweep pain we need to grow beyond the hurt. Processing pain moves us along toward healing and wholeness. It leads us beyond self-centeredness to centering on Christ.

GRIEF

Divorce is a line of demarcation—there's no turning back. The meaning of "divorce" in Greek is "let loose from." Like a potter letting his fingers slip from a clay vessel on a spinning wheel, letting go of intimate relationships leaves deep grooves if not done with care. Divorce produces vile furrows: pent-up anger, guilt, fear, rejection, frustration, hopelessness.

Physical wounds scar the body; emotional wounds scar the soul. If the news of your adult child's divorce dug deep, it's likely you were trying to process the changes too quickly. Because divorce is a great loss, processing takes time. Real grief may not come right away, but after the worst pain is over. And the mourning may take months to work through.

Grieving helps us move along to where we can accept reality, to where we can accept our losses. Parents talk about losses of energy, time, money, privacy. Dreams put on hold. The loss of a romanticized model. For Christian parents, the greatest grief is when their divorced child had not yet discovered the only source of unending love—Christ's love.

Most parents of divorced children go through a stage of mourning, whether they recognize it or not. Disorganized, they are uncertain of their new role: Hands-on parent? Detached friend? Caregiver? Will they become "stand-in parents" to their grandchildren while their adult child retrains, goes to school, or switches professions?

In Linda Weber's book, *Mom, You're Incredible*, the chapter "What Do You Do When Your World Falls Apart?" suggests some ways to hold together as a parent:

Never give up.
Grieve your loss.
Get help.
Cherish your relationships.
Admit your failure and move on.

Keep loving.
Don't dominate.
Be creative.
Let the process refine you.
Stop looking back and wishing.[7]

As a Christian, you are "set apart"—but not separated—from the ravages of sin in the world. Don't waste today's energy on yesterday's heartache. Mourn the losses brought by divorce in your family as quickly and honestly as you can, and then you'll be free to deal with reordering your own life in positive terms.

Read Philippians 4:4–7. In your dark times, focus on thanksgiving and turn your mind toward praise. Let humility realign your thoughts.

SHATTERED EXPECTATIONS

As parents, how much of our own self-interest is caught up in the choices our adult children make? Have we made "idols" out of our ideals? Without a reality check we may have more nightmares than nights of sweet slumber. Parents' expectations need to be filtered through the light of day.

Woody and Nina Newman adore their former daughter-in-law, Glenda. Although they continue a cordial relationship with their son, Mel, they're disappointed with his life choices. They had no warning about his marriage breakup, and only later did they find out he had moved immediately to a live-in liaison.

When the Newmans risked visiting their former daughter-in-law to offer comfort and support, they learned from her that their son's new common-law friend was pregnant—and that it wasn't their son's offspring. Mel had a vasectomy years ago, Glenda told them. His live-in, desperate for a child, had decided on impregnation through a sperm bank. Now Mel is frustrated about raising a child not genetically his own and Woody and Nina wonder what their own relationship to this newborn should be—surrogate grandparents?

The Newmans faithfully raised their children in a Christian context from cradle roll through high school youth camps. They're crushed because their son now marches to a different drum. And they're particularly concerned about the moral milieu surrounding their ten-year-old grandson, who *is* of their biological line.

The triangles in this family crisscross back and forth, intertwining secrets past and present. Mel's sister did not speak to her brother for more than a year after he left his wife. When the divorce was final, family wills were changed left and right. Woody and Nina say it's almost too much to process. "Will we wake up one day from a bad dream?" they ask.

Author Barbra Minar says parents can be "slaves to unrealistic expectations. False expectations . . . steal away our joy." Get in touch with your present emotions, she says. Admit your hurt, fear, worry, and disappointment. "Speak them out to the wind and to God who ordained you a parent. You parent for him. He will show you how to parent, even now."[8]

Here are some beginning points. Recognize that:

Your own feelings count.

You are usually a good parent.

You cannot "fix" your adult child's problems.

Authors Jan and David Stoop define disappointment as "having our dreams frustrated, circumvented, foiled, or ruined." The Stoops recommend the antidote of "disenchantment" to wake us from a fairy-tale view of life. "Disenchantment means we face the truth that a part of our lives was lived in a dream, not in reality," they say. "Disenchantment breaks the chain that binds us so we can dream different kinds of dreams—ones that can be fulfilled."[9]

RENEWED RESPONSIBILITY

Today, midlife parents are challenged to learn how to care for an extended family that encircles multiple marriages, stepchildren, and in-laws—past and present. Most of the parents I talked to found themselves caught up in the backwash when their children divorced. Not only were their children's lives changing, but often their own comfort zones were being disturbed. Understandably, some parents resent the intrusion at this stage of their lives.

"How could she do this to us?! We have our *own* difficulties right now," one couple exclaimed. One father had lost his job through corporate downsizing. Other couples suffered from declining health. Most of these parents were from the "sandwich generation"—with older parents on one end and adult children and their families on the other.

God's nature is revealed in creation. God invites us to share in his nature when we bear children. What does the perspective of "cocreator" mean to you as a parent? Use Colossians 1:9–14 as a prayer petition for your adult children.

Norma cares for her grandchildren in her home three days a week while her divorced daughter works. She finds it hard to also keep up with the needs of her aged mother, who lives alone a few blocks away.

"My mom's mind hasn't been too clear lately," Norma explains. "I have to monitor her medication, help her with meals, and pay bills for her. I can't help her on the days I have the youngsters. And I know I don't have much left to give to my husband after his long day at the pharmacy." Some days it's obvious this wife, mother, grandmother, and adult daughter (all in one person!) doesn't know which end of the family to help first.

Fathers often mention the age of their divorced sons, as if by a certain age they should be immune to personal problems. Midlife dads talk about deferred desires: traveling, relaxing, spending a little of their savings on fun. "It should be my turn to splurge!" they exclaim.

Grandparents now live longer than those in any previous generation—long enough to not only see their firstborn grandchildren, but also to experience the sadness of seeing many young parents of those grandchildren opt for divorce. From sad hearts I heard versions of this refrain: "Parents have no control. You stand by and watch suffering engulf your grown child."

No one said parenting would be easy—at any stage. It isn't. Parenting is one of life's most demanding jobs. Still, parents *know* what to do when their children are little. There are diapers to change, meals to prepare, homework to supervise, a curfew to set. Being a midlife parent can be more frustrating. It requires tact and mature understanding to "not get in the road" of your still-maturing child, yet do the "roadwork" of parenting.

You care about your kids—they are, after all, "bone of your bones, flesh of your flesh." You long for wholeness for them, for you, for the family. But divorce is about disconnection. About the broken links of lineage that lie limp and languid.

"It was tougher than if I were going through it," says Mary Ellen. "It was terrible! Lynette was so brokenhearted, so devastated. She'd hold up at work all day, then come to us and cry and cry. She couldn't cope. I wanted her to accept and go on, but that took four long years."

Write out Psalm 68:19 and put it where you can read it often. Read Psalm 20. Which of these blessings do you want to claim for yourself?

Often, parents admit that, before the divorce, their relationship with their adult child was cordial, but not close. While their adult children were busy with a "life of their own," parents slid along without working on differences or deepening family commitments. Then, during the drought of divorce, the emotional storehouses were drained empty. Old hurts hardened like cement. After all, midlife parents aren't used to an adult child "hanging out" around the house (without warning), wiggling their way into a trip to Hawaii (without invitation), dropping in to do laundry (found the next day, wet and smelly in the washer), or helping himself to drinks and dessert from the fridge.

In your "day of trouble" the Lord will be with you, promises Psalm 20. He daily bears our burdens. Adjusting to change will stretch you. Renewed responsibilities as a parent of a single-again child will test your energy and goodwill. Determine now to focus on the positive in the trying days ahead.

GAINING PERSPECTIVE

A few years ago I took a class in drawing. What I didn't realize was that, with charcoal and sketch pad, I was about to learn something more valuable than just how to transfer images onto paper. I learned about perspective. Looking at something with the naked eye is quite different from isolating that object in a small three-by-five-inch frame, shutting out surrounding distractions. When I put the frame close to an object I saw only a fragment. When I backed off to a better vantage point, the scene took on meaning.

Life is close up right after a divorce in the family; things loom large and out of proportion. At such times, our emotions are "biased and whimsical," says Dobson. "They lie as often as they tell the truth."[10] Emotions are affected by hormones and swayed by physical and mental stress. But if we move our frame of thought toward a heavenly view, jagged pieces begin to fit into a meaningful whole.

Another lesson in perspective comes from my mountain treks. As I wind up the trail with a dozen or so trail mates, gaining elevation and coming to new vantage points, I look back to see our progress. And I look ahead to see our goal, yet higher. That's perspective. That's real life.

As you read this book you may find yourself saying, "If only I'd. . . ." That blind wish is a distorted perspective. You cannot win yesterday's game today. "If you remain focused on the painful experiences in your life, how can there be any joy?"[11] Joy is a peace of inner spirit remaining constant even when life ferments and turns sour.

The following role-playing script telescopes many nights—maybe many weeks—of a mother's prayers. Read it thoughtfully.

Cast: Jane—a distraught mother; narrator—the Holy Spirit

Scene: At home. Midnight or early morning hours. Jane is walking the floor in frustration and prayer.

Jane: For hours I've tried to pray. I begin, "Our Father, which art in heaven. ..." But are you *really* there? Are you God of heaven and earth? How *can* you be and let this divorce happen? It isn't fair! You're supposed to be God of all that is *right!* Right now, it seems everything is all *wrong!*

Carey called tonight to tell us she and Jeremy are divorcing. They've been living apart for three months and haven't said a word about it. "Didn't want to worry you," Carey said. Worry me?! Jim and I had no chance to help. It just can't be so! I'll do anything, God, just tell me what I can do!

Narrator: Jane, you're fighting because you want control. That's a battle you will not win.

Jane: Well, if I can't win, I'll just not fight. I'll believe that Carey and Jeremy won't go through with this. It won't be so.

Narrator: It is so. That's why you rage against it. Unfortunately, Jane, anger is taking over your mind and body. Hate brings destruction, you know.

Jane: But, if only I'd ... sent them on a little vacation, bought them some new furniture, told them how much I love them ... If I'd done something, then this wouldn't be happening. It's *my* fault after all.

Narrator: No, Jane, not your fault at all. You cannot control life. You cannot control your daughter, nor her husband. Jane, you will be comforted when you stop feeling defeated— although you may grieve.

Jane: *(Pleading)* Tell me, how does one grieve?

Narrator: Your sense of loss will be hard to accept for a while. You'll feel depressed at times. The temptation is to give up and give in to despair, to think that nothing is right and good—that there's no hope.

Jane: Now you understand! Yes, I've come to the end of my rope. I have no wisdom. With Job, I dare to ask, "Where does wisdom come from? Where does understanding dwell?"

Narrator: "The fear of the Lord—that is wisdom, and to shun evil is understanding" (Job 28:28). Insisting on control is really selfish, isn't it, Jane? As long as you demand control, you're shutting God out. That's why, Jane, dear, you wonder if he's really there. Give up your obsession to control. Get rid of all bitterness, rage and anger, brawling and slander, along with every form of malice. When you burn out, God will rekindle the flame. Choose either lifelong regret or lifelong praise.

Jane: In trust, I reach out for the hand of God. I surrender my will to you, Lord. I believe you're there, waiting for me. I know you care for me and for my child so quickly grown and gone—gone from me, but not from you. You are in control. Dear Jesus, enfold Carey, and Jeremy too, with my prayers. I pray for both of them. And I pray for myself. I praise you, Jesus. You're the bedrock holding firm my fragile faith. Thank you, Lord, for showing me the folly of my fury. For cooling my rage, lifting my spirit, and leading me back to you. Thank you, God, for "being there" after all.

After reading the dialogue above, think about where you fit in this process. What does the apostle Paul say about grieving the Holy Spirit in Ephesians 4:30–32? Read and reflect on Psalm 19:7–9.

Throughout its pages, this book will urge you to focus on hope. It's possible for parents to build better bridges when the old ones give way. God's love provides the planks. Your family can rebond in new and healthy configurations following divorce. Our darkest hours can usher in untapped inner light. Begin by smiling in the darkness, even when your heart is breaking.

Psalm 139 tells us that before he laid the foundation of the world, God knew you and what you're going through. If you belong to Christ, you're invincibly his—strong enough to face the obstacles. Stand tall. Walk tall. Speak calmly. While you're wondering how to parent again, your own Parent is the "King of kings," the God and Father of us all.

"The greatest promise in all of the Scriptures," says Ruth Graham, "is the 'I am with you' promise."[12] God gives parents strength day by day, along with his peace. God promises never to leave us. In faith, parents can find the solace described in the words of this meditative song:

> *Give him all your tears and sadness,*
> *Give him all your tears of pain,*
> *And you'll enter into life in Jesus' name.*[13]

God does not demand that parents be perfect, only dependable. When we cannot hold back the torrent of divorce in our family, we're faced with walking through it. This book is about surviving in the eye of the storm. Difficulties can turn us toward change and personal growth. They can turn us toward God.

2

GROWING THROUGH THE PAIN

*Help for me? Really? I've been lying awake trying to fig-
ure out how to help my divorced daughter!*

I'll wager you've been talking to yourself a lot these days.
Worrying. Wondering. Hoping. Pondering. Planning. Praying.
Problems don't go away with worry. In fact, problems do not
necessarily go away with prayer. But prayer can transform *you*,
providing you with wisdom and a will to cope.

From the time they are small, children have an uncanny
way of causing you to face the failings in your life. The big question is how to be supportive of your adult child without for-
feiting your own needs or values; how to take an interest in your
adult child and still *take care of yourself.*

START WITH YOURSELF

Your own life is the best place to begin repairs. Maybe
you've been divorced yourself, or you still carry the pain of

being a child of divorced parents. Begin with the way life is now—not the way you wish it were. Take stock of your present relationships with your spouse, with your adult children, and with God. You cannot separate the effect any one of these relationships has on the others.

In *Parenting Isn't for Cowards*, James Dobson reports on a questionnaire sent out by Focus on the Family in which 80 percent of the respondents were women. Their most frequent comment was, "I'm a failure as a mother."[1] What a sad commentary on a lifelong commitment! Having children carries no guarantee. Adult children, especially, can bring grief to their parents.

Giving up is the greatest mistake. As a parent, when you are tempted to identify with failure restock your mind with new ways of thinking and your life with creative ways of relating. Concentrate on bolstering your hope.

Read James 1:5. Where can wisdom
for parenting be found?

Parents of divorced children tend to be hard on themselves. For example, Heddy realized that fretting about her past parenting mistakes—focusing on the "might-have-beens"—caused her to fall into depression. "I had to forgive myself before I could begin to help my son," she explained.

"Doesn't God know it's pouring?" say parents walking with a child through the trials of divorce. Remember, God has planned the physical world—and your life as parents—so you are never without hope. Look for the rainbow in the storm. With God, your world can be set right again so that you can go on.

STRENGTHEN YOUR OWN MARRIAGE BONDS

Even if you've never considered "the big D," your child's divorce may unwittingly cause you to look more critically at your own marriage. A weak hook cannot hold additional weight.

"If our own marriage had not been secure we would have torn apart during our children's upheavals," said one middle-aged mother.

"It was one of the toughest times of our marriage," said a retired dad. "Maybe the toughest of all." A few parents even expressed an honest jealousy that their child had the courage to break out of an unhappy relationship while they, themselves, felt like martyrs in their own marriage.

If your relationship with your spouse has deteriorated over the years—becoming a marriage more of convenience or obligation than love and respect, you may find your adult child's divorce particularly depressing. Is he able to assess reality and move on better than you are? Does it take more courage to divorce than to stagnate, you wonder? These are questions to answer, not avoid.

If your marriage is empty, it's unfair to expect your children, growing or grown, to fill the spaces. When there's a divorce in the family, avoid the temptation to align yourself with your single offspring and neglect your own marriage.

Interaction between husband and wife is sure to accelerate as you take on the burden of a single-again adult child. Avoid blaming your spouse for your adult child's problems. And don't trust your emotions, because sentiments are largely controlled by patterns of the past. One father spouted, "Divorce ages parents like nothing else!"

Take time to consider and agree on plans with your spouse, supporting one another. Be accountable; don't keep secrets. Concealed information isolates you from your mate. And when you stumble in your marriage relationship, quickly ask for forgiveness.

At this time, your need for mutual support is at a high-water mark. Don't judge your spouse by standards of perfection, but by personhood. In between the stress, plan one night a week together when you agree *not* to discuss your adult child and his divorce. Limit daily discussion of your troubles to no more than half an hour.

The best, and most blessed, scenario is that your child's divorce will provide a pivotal time to work on a new solidarity in your marriage. If at all possible, develop a strong union with your spouse, leaving no room for longing to be free from your partnership. In doing so, you'll win in two ways: in your own happiness, and in modeling a spousal relationship where friendship is stronger than discord. A healthy self-love and love between you and your spouse are gifts your adult children appreciate, even if subconsciously.

How do you usually react to stress?
Next time, change your reaction. If you're
a talker, listen. If you always avoid issues,
ask questions. If you usually lose your temper,
count (or pray) silently.

NEW PARENTING ROLES

When divorce comes in your family, don't "grin and bear it," play pretend, or rationalize. False ways of coping do not bring growth. Instead, take the long-range view. Someone has said that life is 10 percent what happens and 90 percent how we respond. God doesn't expect us to be all-good parents. He knows we're human: After all, he made us.

Are you tempted to feel guilty about your adult child's faults, past and present? In *Parents in Pain*, John White says, "All is not lost when our children make foolish choices . . . there is hope when that happens they will learn from experience what they never could have learned from precept."[2]

Unfortunately, we parents seem to think our grown kids are automatically capable of stable living at some designated age we call "maturity." Yet life is not an even measure of maturity because emotional and spiritual maturity may lag behind adult choices such as marriage. Maturity is a lifetime journey.

Although you may have been close before, when your child has a child of her own, you are forced to admit to a new parity. You are both parents now, sharing another cycle of life. A new respect is due. Let God guide your child's life. Hope for the best for him a day at a time and continue to cultivate an adult-to-adult friendship.

Most parents can describe their adult children in graphic terms. But how would you describe *yourself* as a parent of an adult child? Consider these negative images: critic, avenger, troublemaker, doormat, controller. Hopefully, you emulate more positive supportive roles: coach, fan, confidant, friend, encourager.

As I interviewed divorced people, I found emotional fall-out left over from memories of their relationships with their parents when they were adolescents—between ages ten and twenty. *How sad*, I thought, *that one decade dictates a relationship for life!*

I like Larry Stockman's definition of an "egalitarian parent"—"one who values his own needs and feelings as no less and no more important than his child's."[3] The secret of life is coping, not mastering. Write yourself a message and post it as a frequent reminder: Hardships are a healthy part of life—not a sign of bad parenting.

Imperfect people (all of us) can be caring parents. We're merely God's servants; his strength is made perfect in our weakness. There is a caveat, however. A servant cannot dictate the outcome of service. Our grown children may reject our best efforts. Barbra Minar, author of the brochure "Parents in Crisis: Parents in Pain," has some suggestions to help steer parents through foggy swales.

- Be honest. Parents use lots of energy denying and covering up our problems. We need that energy!
- Let our son or daughter know *we* will survive. They need to know we're strong.
- Focus on our own growth and change.
- Take time to enjoy our other children.

- Get help. Reach out to all available resources.
- Trust time. All of us are still in the process of maturation.[4]

Acknowledge the problems you and your family face because of divorce. As you progress through this book, try to honestly assess your options. "Change comes faster and easier if we accept ourselves . . . as people who are doing the best we can. For many of us, just surviving has been an incredible triumph."[5]

CLEAR THE SLATE

We all have our own definition of pain—somewhere between difficult and impossible to endure. If you're so overwhelmed with your own pain that you can't listen well to your adult child's pain, you probably need to clear your own slate.

One mom, stymied by the tempest, searched for a reason, wondering what she had done wrong. Check your mind against the "should-have-dones." Negative thoughts produce blame; positive thoughts produce hope. Replace worries about "what if" with "this is."

But what if you *do* uncover times you wish you could erase? You feel guilty because you traveled a lot or moved the family so often. You remember words hastily spoken or other hurtful actions. How do you erase this guilt?

Say out loud, right now, "I feel guilty about my inadequate ways of relating to (name your son or daughter) in the past." List specific inadequacies, asking God to forgive each one. If you wish, burn the list in a ritual of liberation and thanksgiving. Soon after this, tell your grown child you are going to change some old patterns between the two of you.

As you acknowledge your shortcomings and seek change, share your thoughts with your spouse or a counselor to verify a turning point in your perspective. The best Person to begin talking with is Jesus. Tell him about everything—your fears, doubts, and desires for rebuilding broken bonds. Ask for his wisdom and guidance before you act. Your mind will be refreshed in knowing he listens and understands. He cares; he won't ever let you down. Because of Jesus' love for you, I pray that by the time you turn over the closing pages of this book, you'll be filled with realistic hope.

Society subtly says that the season of life after the kids are gone belongs just to you, for doing the things you've always wanted. Don't be misled. "For you to reduce your life to the tight radius of your own world is not only selfish and unfair to you, it is unfair to your family. . . . God greatly uses crushed and broken vessels!"[6]

Emotionally healthy parents who have cleared their slate find ways to be loving to others without disregarding their own life-stage needs. Lillian's new husband would hold her when she cried because of hurt feelings after a tussle with her divorced daughter, Casey. "I couldn't tell him everything because these problems were not of his making, but he lovingly supported me," she said.

Your adult child knows that you are not perfect. Divorced singles appreciate when their parents are honest about short-comings. You made mistakes in rearing your children to adulthood. That was then; this is now. Failure in one moment in time is not to be doomed forever. Refuse to sink in the quicksand of times past. God's plan for your life is larger than today's viewpoint. Step out of the mire and push ahead.

REBOND YOUR FAMILY

In all my interviews, none duplicated the courage and conviction I saw in the Campbells of Washington, D.C., as they rebonded their family after their daughter's divorce. Even before I flew east from California, I'd heard that the Rev. Campbell and his family were a model of hope and healing.

On a cold December morning I drove north from the capital, leaving the massive stone government buildings behind. Ahead, Tinkertoy-like homes lined littered streets in the rough suburbs. Real families live behind these unkempt facades, I reminded myself. Probably, in many of the narrow, pastel town-houses, several families huddle together, sharing a single unheated bathroom and an outmoded kitchen. Along a main street, I found the Campbells' chunky red-brick church.

Perhaps it had been a day like that day, windy and blustery, when Shana and her four-month-old child, Justin, moved back home to D.C.

In group study, assign parts and role-play the following script of this family's model recovery.

Cast: Pastor Campbell—balding, middle-aged; daughter Shana—composed young mother; interviewer—seeking information for a book

Scene: Pastor Campbell is seated at his desk in his church office underneath a handcarved sign proclaiming: "No Surprises Here!" The interviewer is seated in front of the desk. Shana walks in, wraps her arms around her father's shoulders, and gives him a light kiss on his balding forehead, then sits down.

Campbell: *(Glowing with pride)* Shana is the bright spot in my life. But it wasn't always so. Shana's marriage breakup was my first encounter with divorce in our extended family. I was tempted to give in to shame. But image and ego had to go. When I faced the divorce head-on and was honest with my congregation, one member said, "Welcome! You're one of us now."

Shana: My parents never said "I told you so." I appreciated that. Instead they loved me according to my needs.

Interviewer: What were some of those needs, Shana?

Shana: Well, mom and dad added a kitchen to the first level of their home so my son, Justin, and I could have our own place to live.

Campbell: I couldn't let my daughter and grandson move out on the streets. Dorcas, my wife, and I wanted to know that they were safe at night.

Interviewer: *(To Campbell)* How did you go about inviting Shana into your home?

Campbell: When Shana's marriage collapsed, I called a family conference. I apologized for intruding, but I told Shana she was welcome to come home—if that was her choice.

Shana: Funny thing about it was that my mother-in-law, Myrna, who lived with my ex-husband and me, asked if she could come too.

Campbell: I was afraid that having three adult women in one house might cause problems. But I left the decision up to Shana.

Shana: It turned out that having Myrna living with us was a gift from God. I didn't have to worry about my son's care. My mom works as a nurse, so Myrna faithfully took care of Justin so I could work and also go back to school.

Campbell: *(Smiling)* We, of course, were quite careful what we said about our former son-in-law! Myrna and Dorcas became the best of friends—like sisters. In many ways, Myrna made up for all that her son didn't do. She lived with us until her death.

Interviewer: Did Shana pay rent?

Campbell: Dorcas and I talked about that—as we do about all family decisions. Although that was ideal, we learned that Shana's ex had left her with enormous credit-card debts. So it seemed enough to expect Shana to pay those. She did, too—even without child support.

Shana: Dad sometimes gave me money, but not just to be generous or make me feel good. It had to be for a real need.

Interviewer: Was it easier for your family to be close-knit because of ethnic conditioning?

Campbell: *(Thoughtfully)* I think it's more because we know we're part of the family of God. We have forgiveness that comes from Christ's love. I can get angry easily. When I saw what was happening to my daughter and grandson, I could have been mean. I had to let God overrule my stubborn heart.

Interviewer: What do you tell other parents who feel pain after one or more of their adult children divorce?

Campbell: *(Pensively)* When divorce hits it's a parent's responsibility to continue to love even when the adult child is breaking your heart. In our pain, all we could do was pray. And we've seen a wonderful transformation! Shana has lost her rebellious attitude. She's become tender and loving and a joy to have as an adult daughter. We loved her then . . . we love her now.

Shana: *(Softly)* Thank you, Jesus.

Read Hebrews 12:12–15. What qualities allowed this family to succeed in helping their divorced daughter and grandson?

LIGHTEN UP!

When you feel squeezed until you're wrung out, lighten up. Learn to laugh. Find the humorous side—or create one. If you're basically a joyous person, your hurting adult child will catch your spirit.

"Blessed are the flexible" is an apt beatitude for parents. The malleable parent assesses his strengths and weaknesses. He is able to accept rejection because his trust is rooted in Christ, who is steadfast. "Each time I turned a corner, I came upon some new stage I wasn't expecting," explained a mom who has seen three divorces in her family. She assured me she's still learning.

Popular speaker Barbara Johnson puts the reality of life's struggles in graphic terms. "First we churn, burn, yearn." Finally, we "learn and turn."[7] For parents whose adult children have divorced, "turning" will include rebuilding family bonds.

Here are some pointers to get you started down the well-traveled path of survival and wholeness:

- Keep reasonably busy with things unrelated to your adult child's life (not so busy that you're truly unavailable, just busy enough to balance out your negative emotions).

- Keep physically fit; enjoy a pleasurable hobby.
- Strengthen supportive relationships through common interests, study, and prayer.
- Get all the help you need—from clergy, doctor, or therapist—so you can cope.
- Keep a journal of your thoughts and feelings.

Being at peace with yourself and your marriage is a prerequisite for being at peace with your troubled adult child. Parenting is risky business, says author Ruth Senter. "Sometimes it means acting on the gentle nudges of the Holy Spirit even when there are no clear-cut reasons. . . . For risk is not risk until it is willing to lose everything to keep what is most important."[8]

If, instead of risking, you just tighten your grip on the past, you'll shrivel in fear of the unknown. Meet change head-on. For example, make allowances for new family unions. If you leave an inheritance to a grandchild who dies while your former in-law has custody, that parent could collect. Reviewing your will now may save you grief later. While you're doing it, consider writing out and including a "statement of faith" to pass on as a priceless part of your heritage.

When faced with sorrow, the teachable parent affirms herself and slices through stress with a gracious spirit. She believes Christ is at work in her for ultimate good. The resourceful parent plants her own garden and decorates her own soul; she doesn't wait for someone else to bring her flowers.

IF YOU NEED IT, GET HELP

Few parents purposely fail. Like most of us, you had high hopes for your family. In *How to Eat Humble Pie & Not Get Indigestion*, Charlene Baumbich talks about humility as a voluntary surrender to God: "A lot of growth comes through humility . . . it is only when you absolutely can't take any more of where you're going that you grow!"[9]

Don't keep "beating up on yourself" or feel guilty if you occasionally slip back into the old pits of anger and depression.

As you flex emotional muscle, each climb upward will become easier. You want to be a victor, not a victim, in the unrest of divorce in the family.

Through the years you watched your children grow physically. Now they need to watch you grow—emotionally and spiritually. Your problems are different from those of your divorced child. Are you holding onto their wounds as if they were your own? Instead, ask the Lord, "What do you want me to learn from all this?" No one is too old to change an attitude—to change their heart. Allow the Great Artist to paint his portrait in your life. Claiming God's love for yourself is the best way to have it handy for your hurting divorcee.

Life's good times don't last forever, but neither do the bad. God gave us feelings so we could work our way through circumstances, not let them crush us.

In a group, or alone with a friend, you may not be able to talk about your thoughts without crying. That's okay. In fact, it's healthy—as long as you cry with someone who empathizes with your pain. A good cry can check angry impulses. Shared tears help us accept feelings and bring inner release.

And when you shout, "Help!" reach out and grasp God's hand. There is help. There is hope. As the Rev. Robert Schuller has said, we can turn scars into stars. But take warning! This requires both soul-searching and serious self-appraisal. "Self is who you really are. Self-image is who you think you are. Who we are determines our destiny, but who we think we are determines the way we live today."[10]

REMEMBER, TESTING DEVELOPS PERSEVERANCE

There's a post-a-note on my bathroom mirror reminding me of three important questions I ask myself each day: *What am I happy about? Whom do I love? Who loves me?* Then, I find one *specific* thing to look forward to that day. I remember how much I love my husband, my adult children, and my bevy of grandchildren. I say their names—out loud. Before I turn toward the day, I affirm: "God loves me." And in his amazing grace, I'm also able to say: "I love you, too, ML. Have a nice day."

When we hurt physically, we seek a prescription that works over a period of time. Cures—whether for physical or emotional pain—are not instantaneous. In time, we can be strengthened by healing grace. Every ending is also a new beginning: Divorce is a dissolution, but it can also be a portal to a deeper Spirit-filled journey. Speaker Chuck Swindoll says reality forces every Alice out of her Wonderland and into God's Wonderful Plan.

Post-divorce can be an excellent opportunity to help your adult child (and perhaps yourself) deal with "unfinished business." "Parents are essentially modeling the characteristics of God in the way they treat their children," says author-speaker Kay Moore. "That can be good if they learn love, support and praise."[11]

Your adult child has chosen—or been pushed into (whichever way you see it)—the world of divorced singles. His marriage didn't work. But instead of condemning, help your son make his divorce work. Like a novice swimmer, he may flounder for a time. Yet, many parents I interviewed told me how their child's life-stroke was stronger after pushing through the deep waters of divorce. That's encouraging!

When Paul was newly divorced, he told his sister, "Everyone else's life just goes on as usual—no one seems to notice that mine has fallen apart." Many months later, his parents, Krista and Larry, heard Paul joking around with his sister: "We were so pleased," said Krista. "It had been a long time since we'd heard Paul laughing and enjoying himself. It was a true sign of healing." Divorced adults want parents who can help them see the "finish line." That's where you can stand tall and reach out to grab their hand. As they stumble through each day, they're looking for holy stability and the human touch.

I recall the day my one-year-old daughter took her first steps. I watched, but did not reach out. Sure, she might fall, but if she made it she would know *she* did it—not I. If she wanted reassurance, her body language would tell me that. I was careful not to stifle her fledgling spirit.

As our adult children face the emotional riptides of divorce, their steadiness is challenged. But, like their toddler days, they need to reach the "other side" on their own two feet. Just knowing a parent is standing by—within reach—is more than enough reassurance. Maybe they'll take a tumble. Most adults do. They'll try again if they don't lose hope. I encourage you to give the gift of hope to your injured adult child—and to yourself.

"Today is the first day of the rest of your life," proclaims a popular poster. It's never too late to be a better parent. Life's camcorder is running, capturing the moment and panning the future. Yesterday is a canceled check; tomorrow, a promissory note. Today is cash!

Prayer, patience, and love lessen the hurt. "God's mercies are new every morning," assures the psalmist. The flower from the seed; in the kernel of faith, new life.

3

LISTENING TO YOUR DIVORCED SON OR DAUGHTER

Long ago, when your toddler fell down you rushed to hold him and ask, "What happened?" You hoped the facts would unfold between his heaving cries. Finally you realized that even if you *knew* what happened, it wouldn't change the present situation. It was time for calming.

When an adult child falls and fails in marriage, it's not the time to ask, "What happened?" or "Whose fault is it?" The pain is more than skin-deep; the wounds are internal. The anguish goes way down to the pit of her stomach and carves a hole in her heart. A Band-Aid won't make it all better.

The days of mending skinned knees are long gone. You're older now. Your divorced child is twenty-five, maybe thirty-five. She's been gone from home five, ten, fifteen years. In many ways she's a different person. I sometimes see bumper stickers that say, "It's 10 P.M. Do you know where your teenager is?" In ten years, I wonder if that same parent will be saying: "It's the twenty-first century, do I know *who* my adult child is?"

Even if you may feel professionally inferior to a son or daughter who has climbed the corporate ladder or who is more technically skilled than you are, you can still be an island of calm in the eye of a storm simply because you've been through more of life's traumas. If you know yourself well, enjoy your strengths and accept your weaknesses, get along well with others, and live each day in faith, you have wisdom to offer, even to an M.D. or Ph.D. son or daughter.

In this chapter you may hear things you've wanted to know but feared to ask your divorced child. Listen to the advice culled from scores of singles with whom I talked. Most were quite candid about their relationship to their parents. Some told me how their parents are part of the answer to their problems. Others, unfortunately, believe their parents are still part of their problems.

"DON'T REJECT ME"

Breaking the news about a marriage breakup is one of the most distressing things adult children unload on parents. They put off telling their parents about their marital problems because they don't want to admit to failure. Marie hung onto a bad marriage during her mother's lifetime for fear of recrimination. "It would have killed my mother to see me get a divorce," she says softly.

Another woman, Carol, recalls her mother's off-the-cuff reaction to her second failed marriage: "Well, I guess you're going to be a two-time loser!" Carol's mother was embarrassed and concerned about what her friends would say and think about *her*.

Amy says it wasn't easy to call her mother with news that her marriage of two decades had ended. "After I told my mom that I was alone, there was a long, uncomfortable pause. Then she callously asked, "Have you gone on a diet yet?" Amy couldn't believe that her mother was already wondering how her daughter might attract another man. "How could I explain that I wasn't able to eat *anything*, was waking up with dry heaves and even contemplating suicide? I firmly told my mom never to bring up my appearance again!"

Martha's parents have never spoken of Martha's divorce, which happened years ago. "Their rejection made me ill," Martha states. "I don't see that my relationship with either of my parents has any hope of changing. I don't hate my mother. I just don't want her in my life."

Erika says that it took her two and a half years to tell her mother (who lived in Germany) about her divorce. When Erika so much as even thought about telling her mother, she would get diarrhea or a headache. "I was born from a love affair," says Erika, "and my mother never became the bride. She never let go of living out her dream through me. My wedding fulfilled her fantasies. My marriage had to be good! But it wasn't, although I had hoped so too. I believe that my divorce forced my mother to finally admit her own failures. She couldn't handle the hurt, so she has chosen to not talk about it."

Some divorced children feel that telling their parents in person about their broken marriages would be too painful, so they write to them instead. But Charlene didn't write until she had tried—and failed—to talk with her parents.

After draining her bank account and exhausting precious vacation time, Charlene flew several states away to tell her parents she had left a marriage so stressful that her health was endangered. "For four days I tried to tell them my story," says Charlene, "but my mother only talked *at* me about 'being submissive,' about 'paying no mind to other's faults,' about 'giving the devil no room.' I never had a chance to explain what I'd been through in that destructive relationship—that I needed to be free to survive. I came back home and wrote my parents a long letter. I can still feel their condemnation."

Naomi also wrote to her parents to tell them about her divorce. But they never mentioned the subject in subsequent phone calls. Naomi says, "Even a year later when I went to visit,

I could tell by my dad's face he still didn't want to talk about it." This single woman longs to be emotionally closer to her father.

Never hearing "I told you so!" from parents means a lot to a divorced adult. A woman from Texas says, "My mother couldn't accept that I had failed at marriage. It's like she thinks I didn't try. I prayed hard that my marriage would make it, but it didn't. Parents want respect, but they seem to forget that respect flows both ways. It's those put-downs that keep things unsettled between my mother and me."

If you feel that your son or daughter's divorce is a life failure, why do you feel the way you do? Be objective.

In my survey I suggested a dozen images that might describe a divorced adult's relationship to his or her parents. Four to one chose negative images such as "stormy seas," "bumper cars," "king and peon," "political lobby," and "front lines." Positive descriptions, such as "refreshing oasis" and "sunny sailing," trailed behind. Yet, when asked to choose a number between one (worst) and ten (best) that represented their relationship with their parents, most chose seven, eight, nine, and even ten! Apparently, even though singles choose dissonant terms to describe their parental relationship, they still want to believe the best possible. They want to feel that they're accepted for who they are—apart from being like mom or dad.

What else is your divorced son or daughter saying?

"LOVE AND CHERISH ME"

The stress of divorce causes people to be somewhat disoriented for awhile. Hearing your daughter say, "I feel like I'm dead and walking around" or "I feel like breaking everything" is frightening, but normal. Such strong statements reflect her journey through the grieving process: denial, bargaining, anger, depression, and reluctant acceptance. Give her permission to get the grief out. Affirm her feelings while you watch for break-throughs. Even small bits of progress carry hope.

"I want my mom (dad) to care about me," is a composite response to my survey. And more than one divorced person added a wish that parents would "soothe my spirits when I don't make it."

"My mother gives compliments with one hand and criticism with the other," says Amy. "I almost never feel affirmed around her." Parents who see their adult children as they are give them a priceless gift. No matter their age or how successful they are, most grown children yearn to love their parents and long to feel cherished.

Put yourself in your child's place. Your son may be looking for the love and security he didn't find in an unhappy marriage. Now, after divorcing, he wonders if he'll ever love and trust anyone. To him, you are a "power person" who still wields influence, helping or hindering him. Your willingness to risk believing in him goes a long way toward his healing. It may open his heart to God's sustaining love.

"GIVE ME TIME"

Parents are usually too anxious for their divorced children to get back to normal. Moms and dads who understand that post-divorce recovery is a process that can be helped, but not hurried, are the ones most appreciated.

Although they may keep a stiff upper lip, divorced adults have been through one of life's most traumatic tragedies. They've suffered rejection, perhaps violence—at the least, hate. They probably endured many nights of heartache before their parents even knew there were severe problems in their marriage. Only the death of a spouse is more traumatic than divorce, and grief over death may not last as long as grief in the aftermath of divorce. Your adult child needs time to deep heal.

Rhonda admires her parents, who allowed her "emotional space" to regroup in her life. After the divorce they told her to use this time of her life to sort through life's meaning. "Women, particularly, need to feel that they 'can do,'" says Rhonda, now an ordained pastor. "In just everyday things my parents affirm me. I can still hear them saying, 'It's going to be hard, but it's not the end of the world.' I made it through those years, partly because of their consistent encouragement."

Nichole likes taking long walks with her octogenarian dad and talking about soul matters. She muses: "My dad's saintliness and goodness have been an inspiration to me, especially since my divorce. Whenever we spend time together his warmth enfolds me."

"DON'T TRY TO SOLVE MY PROBLEMS"

In my interviews with divorced adults, a common complaint was that parents attempt to "take over." I heard similar stories about how parents try to manipulate them into becoming dependent children again—no matter what their age.

Parents need to ask if they're creating more problems for their adult children, or intensifying those that exist. For example, Martha kept telling her daughter that she had a *right* to a new automobile in her divorce settlement. Martha's daughter, who had already agreed about the division of property, was emotionally stirred up by her mother's judgments.

Do you interject your opinion to relieve your *own* feelings? Before you do, think. Will your comments truly help, or only agitate your adult child? Be sympathetic but as noninvolved as possible with arrangements regarding visitation, finances, and other settlement issues between the former couple.

When your adult child focuses on being the "victim" in the web of divorce settlement, ask questions that help him clarify what can be done, and what cannot. Refrain from offering solutions. Ultimately, your son must accept his new status. Jim Smoke, a pastor to singles, says that divorced persons choose to "go through" or to "grow through" the rebuilding of their lives.

Since divorce occurs most often during the first seven
years of marriage, younger single-again adults usually
expressed that they needed help from their birth family. But the
kind of support they wished for was to be friends, to not argue
so much, to be affirmed in their own parenting. They didn't
want their parents to solve their problems for them.

Singles complained that their parents lacked perception
and understanding, and failed to work through conflicts with
them. I heard descriptions of mothers "coming on too strong"
about what divorced singles should or should not do. Fathers
were described as nonreactive; or, if they did react, as being
judgmental. A divorced Asian woman whose father had not
come to her wedding because it was a mixed marriage says,
"My father was stoic when I told him I was going to be divorced,
but I could see the crow's feet form on his forehead. In Man-
darin, he kept mumbling, 'I tried to tell you.'"

"LISTEN TO *ME* FOR A CHANGE"

"How easily can you talk with your parents about things
that matter to you?" I asked divorced singles in an informal survey. "Hardly at all," was the weighted response.[1]

Amy said, "I'm always on guard around my mother. I work
hard to keep her from constantly upsetting my apple cart. But,
occasionally, I get caught in her manipulative net. On the phone
recently, my mom sweetly said, 'How are you, dear?' When I
told her that I was miserable and worried, she responded, 'So
what have you done *now* to get yourself in such a mess?' I flat-
out told her, 'I'm frustrated when you jump to the conclusion
that I'm the one at fault.'

"Then I told her that my hours had been cut back at work
and I was concerned about being financially able to keep the
house. I tell you, sometimes I wonder if it's worth 'parenting'
my parent."

Over and over I heard that parents best help their divorced
adult by asking thought-provoking questions, not by giving

answers. Most reflected Norman's view: "I want my parents to talk *with* me, not *at* me."

After his divorce, Norman moved from the East to the West Coast to put distance between him and his family's constant criticisms. "They made me feel responsible for *their* hurt," he analyzes. "On the one hand they'd say, 'Poor Baby, he doesn't have his kids now.' On the other hand they said I'd have to pay back one half of the money they had put up on our home. My parents never asked about how I was feeling on the *inside*. I wanted to tell them that I was feeling numb—like a hopeless failure."

For a long time after her divorce, Karen called her mom every day—long distance. "I knew she would listen. She understood; she'd been divorced, too. I needed to hear her say, 'You're going to get through this and be a lot stronger.'" Karen would cry over the phone and her mom would cry with her. Often Karen's mom would end their call with, "God's going to see you through."

Although Bart didn't appreciate an aunt who read him Scripture over the phone, he did appreciate phone chats with his mom. "She *asked* me if I felt like talking before broaching personal stuff," he said. Bart's needs drew him closer to his mother. "I didn't even resist when she suggested that I read the Psalms for consolation—I'm glad I tried it."

"TREAT ME LIKE THE ADULT I AM"

"I finally told my mom that I just wouldn't be treated like a five-year-old anymore!" says Jana, as she gingerly navigated slippery rocks, mud puddles, and dense patches of tall wild oats, grown waist high during the past rainy winter. Jana and I were scurrying down Mount Figueroa in the Santa Ynez Valley in an unexpected rainstorm. As we wound down the narrow trail, Jana talked about her recent divorce and about how her folks were dealing with it.

Married for a quarter of a century, Jana, now in her midforties, had reared both children and stepchildren. "My mom is planning my life again—do this, do that. She's sure that I need her now more than ever! She never asks me what I want or need. There's nothing like a parent to make you feel like a child!"

"What about your dad, Jana? Can you talk with him?"

"Not really. Dad no longer thinks that what he says matters. Mom runs the family show. Since retirement, he just hides behind his newspaper and golf clubs."

Although Jana's mother wants to be a confidante, she has instead become an antagonist. And Jana's dad has given in and given up. Jana is determined to escape the well-worn intergenerational pattern; she simply doesn't tell her parents about her life.

What caused Jana to exclaim in frustration, "There's nothing like a parent to make you feel like a child!" In what ways can you affirm your divorced child?

A divorced woman from Arkansas sums up the feelings I heard from various singles: "Divorce was an embarrassment to my parents. They loaded me with a sense of shame. I don't think my parents know how to relate to me anymore. I wish they could get to know me as I am *now*, not as they remember me as a child, or what they think I *should* be like. There's healing and hope for those who are divorced, but my folks can't see that."

You've always interpreted your son or daughter's personality through *your* eyes and *your* temperament. But how is he seen by his friends and colleagues? If possible, ask for a tour of his workplace. Read one of his professional journals. Finding out what it takes for him to repair a car engine, paint a house, or sell vacuums may give you a new appreciation of who he is as an adult.

If you are reading this book in a group, for variety you may wish to videotape some of the many role-plays prior to your meetings. Pairs of characters, such as the father and son in the following skit, might reverse roles and retape. Show the short film and share with the group your feelings as you played the parts. In the scenario below, what attitude adjustment does the father need for a good adult-adult relationship with his son? (Read Proverbs 3:35).

Cast: Divorced son, his father
Scene: Parents' living room

Son: Dad, I was wondering if you would consider giving me a loan for a good car deal I saw last Saturday.

Father: There has never been a "good" car deal! *Where* was it? *What* kind of a car, anyway?

Son: My boss gets his cars at Chrome City. He's been pleased. This is really a good buy on a late model Ventura, low mileage, good tires, clean . . .

Father: You just started working at Global Computers this year. Already you want to buy cars like your boss. Do you know how many years I had to work to buy a car when I was your age?

Son: Dad, just forget that I asked, okay?

Father: Remember you have hefty child support payments now that you're divorced. I can't support you and your family, you know. By the way, how much is the car?

Son: The asking price is only $15,000, but I'd have some trade-in.

Father: That's a ridiculous price! You must think I'm made of money! I guess, since you need money, your job isn't so good after all. Or maybe you're spending too much having fun instead of saving your hard-earned money. I tell you, I learned to save as soon as I had a paycheck.

Son: If I decide to make an offer on the car, I'll try to finance it at the bank.

Father: You know your credit isn't good enough for that. No bank will take a risk on a single parent with kids. I'd have to *give* you the money before you could even talk about owning a new car.

Son:	I didn't ask you to give me any money. I was talking about a loan.
Father:	Same difference. You never know for sure that you'll ever see a penny of it when you loan money to a child.
Son:	Yeah . . . I'm the child . . . you're the father. I'll have to let you decide what is best for me.

How might this interchange have been handled more amicably? How do you help your divorced child think through choices?

"JUST BE THERE"

A divorced person's well-being seems not to be affected by their own stress (at least not after the initial blow) as much as by lingering stress within their own family circles. The most essential ingredient in parenting a grown child can be expressed in two words: *Be there.*

Just "being there" is a difficult part to play, especially when the hurting one is your own grown child. Hang in there with what author-pastor Walter Wangerin Jr. calls "holy stability and the human touch. . . . The Griever, who suffered the sundering of relationship, needs relationship. You [as a comforter] are her life. It requires only your proximate bodies, eyes unafraid to gaze at her, arms willing to hug her when she thinks she's about to fly apart, hands to touch her, kindness. Kindness."[2]

Hands-on help is practical kindness. Volunteer to mend clothes, check out apartments to rent, type a resume, wrap gifts, and chauffeur grandkids. Do whatever you can that you feel good about doing. Offer specific help, but don't take over.

Divorced singles long for autonomy, yet need to know they can depend on their parents when needed. For example, Linda found her distraught mother growing weary from doing too much for her two divorced daughters. Linda helped by being very specific about needs. "I asked my mom to come once a week to baby-sit on my group-recovery night. She would stay over, and the next morning we had time for coffee and conversation after the kids left for school. I grew closer to my mom, and she was being helpful without an overload."

Many adults that I interviewed talked about how they appreciated help from various extended family. Brothers moved furniture and helped them buy a car. Sisters invited them to parties and took care of their children. Extra money was sometimes tucked into notes of encouragement from aunts, uncles, and grandparents.

Annette, a woman who lived in England at the time of her divorce, was glad her parents paid for her sister to fly from Minneapolis to London. "I couldn't think straight and had many decisions to make. My family knew that Juliet and I had always been close and she'd be the one I could relate to most easily. Frankly, having my parents come would have been more of a burden than a help."

Karen, who was facing a third divorce, remembers how hard it was to call and tell her dad that she was suffering physical abuse. "If he hadn't said, 'Come home,' I'd probably have committed suicide," Karen says, her voice cracking from the memories of her duress. "I felt that I'd failed again—dying seemed the only way out."

Karen explained that although her dad had never said, "I love you," he showed his love in telling her to "just leave your personal belongings behind and come; nothing else is as important as you!" "It meant so much to know that my dad was there for me . . . he truly cared. He didn't have to give me things, just his love."

"I NEED CHRISTIAN COMPASSION"

Divorced adults had some revealing things to say about the church's reaction to their single status. Colton, a music director in a large congregation, remembers how difficult it was at the time of his marriage breakup to sit through sermons that proclaimed: "If you are righteous, the Lord will put your marriage together again." Now divorced, Colton feels that his life is much more together. But harsh words from the pulpit caused him to question his faith for a time. "Then I saw that faith wasn't the issue. Divorce is a broken relationship between two imperfect people," he says.

One woman recalls phone calls and letters from church leaders who told her, "You can't do that!" when her divorce was in progress. "They weren't in my shoes," she says. Another woman recalls a priest's reaction to her request for counseling: "I'm busy. You go home and pray. God will take care of you." Hurt and angry, she left the church for several years.

Most new singles church-shop to meet their life-stage needs.

"In one church, when I asked if there was an adult singles group, people looked shocked and said, 'Of course not!'" reports a divorced woman.

Other divorced singles had thoughts about how the church might be helpful rather than hurtful. "The church can be a substitute family," says one forty-year-old single mom with three teenagers. "A loving group can see you through. I think more singles need to ask people in the church to pray for them."

Sometimes divorced adults want their parents to see how God helped them rebuild their lives. Norman, a new Christian, says his parents know he's changed and that visits with them are calmer now. Norman talks about how divorce intensified his spiritual quest. Smiling, he says, "In my recovery from divorce, I've found the *real me.*"

Small covenant groups helped some divorced adults look at life with new perspective. In these groups they identified with other divorced persons, felt affirmed, and were held accountable for recovery. Singles didn't expect their pastor to counsel with them more than a few times. They agreed that professional counselors are better for long-term help.

Bernadette, who had a mission to organize African-American divorcees, had her church's support. Her local priest told her, "God gave you life; you are giving it back to him. You do whatever he leads you to do."

This young black woman empathized with the singles in her divorce recovery groups who came from several different denominations. "Some of their parents were telling these singles, 'You'll go to hell because you're divorced' and 'You disgrace our family,'" Bernadette said. "If God forgives me—and I believe he does—then I hope my parents and my church can forgive me too. Their forgiveness helps me to move on.

"Divorce is not the worst thing that's happened in my life. Hard as it was, it was also a new spiritual beginning for me. If I hadn't gone through those days I wouldn't be the person I am today. We're never too old to learn, and I've learned to look at life from God's perspective," Bernadette concludes.

"PARENTS WHO CARE"

At the altar, young people hope they have found "true love forever." Then, divorce proves that even married love is fragile. "Who will love me forever?" your single wonders. "Ah, my parents; surely the ones who gave me life still love me!" Parents of divorced sons and daughters are in a unique position to model Christ-like love and to point their grown children to the only secure love in all of life: a relationship with Jesus himself.

That sounds like Bernadette's very words: "God is the Ultimate Parent. I find my strength in him. He is real. He's Someone I talk to each day. He's so much more than my parents could ever be—as wonderful as they are."

What would divorced people like to tell their parents? Ponder these responses:

- My dreams
- How much I hurt
- How I felt about their parenting as I was growing up
- Not to judge me as a wayward adolescent

Author Jim Conway says, "When emotional baggage is being carried by both parent and a grown child, they are worse than strangers—there's negative history to deal with."[3] I agree. But in reconciliation there is hope. Determine to listen better.

To love more. In twenty years of writing about family life I've come to the conclusion that, with prayer and good counseling, caring parents and their grown children can be much closer. May it be so for you and your single adult child.

4

STAYING IN TOUCH WITH YOUR SINGLE-AGAIN CHILD

Like Humpty Dumpty, you can't put your child's marriage back together again. Neither can you fill the emotional needs of your single adult. As your newly divorced child begins to rebuild, parents should act as assistant carpenters, not contractors—available, but not intrusive. No matter how free-spirited your adult child may seem, she still needs her parents' love and trust. Author Sharon Marshall expresses the anguish of the divorced: "I don't need your words. I need your presence; I need your love. Cry with me. Make me laugh. Sit with me in silence—but, *please* don't desert me."[1]

With what sort of relationship do you begin? Have you been the analyzer of her every choice, or have you avoided talking about her real concerns? Maybe you've been the polite parent, keeping an even keel. Or perhaps you can remember plenty of conflict. There has most likely been a pattern. Is it a healthy one, full of acceptance and truth? Take an honest inventory.

Research differs on whether moms or dads are more likely to accept—even enjoy—having their adult children be somewhat dependent after a divorce in the family. Some reports say a mother feels useful and needed again. Others say just the opposite, that moms resent having to "go backward," giving up their midlife freedom to be concerned about children they thought were grown and gone.

Writers slot dads in opposite pockets, too. Some say, compared to mothers, they are more humiliated by a son or daughter's divorce. It's a sign of failure. They expected more out of their offspring—success all the way! Others say that dads, maybe under a stoic facade, are glad to have a "second chance" to parent again. In midlife, men may regret earlier emotional losses. They're anxious to absolve themselves for not having spent more time with their young children and feel they'll do better relating to a single adult child, and enjoy it more.

DADS, DAUGHTERS, AND SONS

"For the majority of daughters it's important to try to reconnect with their father in adulthood: to get to know their father once and for all—in ways they didn't in childhood, or adolescence, or even young adulthood—and to reframe their relationship beyond blame and outmoded dreams."[2] This reconnecting is particularly meaningful to a divorced woman who, without it, may continue to look for a substitute father in a future marriage.

A father who is manipulative or demands control taints his daughter's image of masculinity. She is likely to attract another man who will continue to manipulate her. Conversely, a father's affirmation can renew a daughter's confidence dispelled by divorce. As she senses paternal approval and acceptance, she is set free to measure her own competence, intelligence, and self-worth in relation to other men.

Although writing to fathers of teenage daughters, psychologist Norman Wright gives suggestions for a healthy relationship that could also apply to a divorced daughter in her twenties or thirties:

- Accept her values.
- Encourage her femininity and sexuality.
- Encourage her potential.
- Let her see your emotional side.
- Take time to communicate with her.
- Involve yourself in her life.
- Give her space to grow.
- Demonstrate a healthy family role model.
- Nurture her self-esteem and identity.[3]

In *Always Daddy's Girl*, Dr. Wright shows how each of these areas is significant in the father's relationship with a grown daughter. He suggests that fathers release their daughters to make their own life choices. As a gift, Wright recommends a father's handwritten letter to his grown daughter—now a woman in her own right—telling her how special she still is to him.

Sons, too, shocked by the loss of married love and relationship, need a father's affirmation. Dr. Charles Scull believes that many men are hungry for male role models as they become aware of "their inward weeping for the fathers they hardly knew." They're seeking, he says, "to understand in the deepest sense what it is to be a man."[4] Scull outlines three meaningful things a man can learn from his father (or grandfather): discipline, worldly wisdom, and the importance of lineage.

The typical father's reaction, especially when a son divorces, is disappointment. "When I was in my early thirties," says one father, "I had a good job and was supporting a family. Here's Jim, back at home with child-support payments, unable to make it on his own. It's depressing. Not only does he feel like a failure; somehow, I do too."

A son may have grown up believing he should share only successes so his father won't be disappointed in him. Then comes a momentous failure—divorce. A father can help a struggling son see that expressing honest emotions doesn't necessarily mean losing control. If a son can share his feelings with his dad without fearing rejection, it goes a long way toward establishing a nonthreatening and healing trust.

MOMS, SONS, AND DAUGHTERS

The major premise of *Between Mothers and Sons*, by Evelyn S. Bassoff, is that mothers help sons become vital and loving men by respecting their unique, separate, male lives. The practice of respect, however, requires an enormous dedication to awareness, tolerance, knowledge, and understanding. For most mothers, showing such respect is a conscious effort, "a difficult maternal labor,"[5] writes Bassoff.

There's a maternal pull to rush to the aid of a son struggling in the strong wake of divorce. We want to grab hold and haul him to safe ground. But rescuing him deprives a son of the maturing experience of humbly facing problems and, in a realistic way, becoming a stronger, emotionally healthier, and spiritually stable man.

Read Romans 12:9–10. How can the phrase "honor one another above yourselves" apply to your relationship with your divorced son or daughter?

Both mothers and sons profit from personal stories of conviction and courage. Your son is probably more interested than you think he is in knowing how you've faced insecurities and fears, and also what your faith meant to you during those times. While it's not wise for a mother to share the particulars of her sexual life, many other aspects of her emotional life may be both appropriate and helpful to share. Says Bassoff: "Isn't it time for many of us to remove the 'giant mask of motherhood' that muffles the words of the woman hidden behind it and to tell our sons stories that represent us?"[6]

A son wants to preserve a positive, loving image of his mother. And the best climate for sharing is trust. "When a son loses trust in his mother, it is as if he has lost part of himself."[7] A mother's level of trust with her son affects his ability to trust other women in his life, especially another potential life partner.

Typically, it's easier for a mother to talk to her daughter than her son. After all, they share not only a common physique, but a feminine perspective. Emotional closeness is important to most women, so mothers are especially sad when bonds are broken with a daughter. But too often mothers, in a martyr role, take the blame for severed ties.

In *Don't Blame Mother: Mending the Mother-Daughter Relationship*, Paula Caplan's goal is to help mothers and daughters understand the barriers between them. Often a mother's "way of thinking" is particularly critical of her divorced daughter's choices as a single. Mothers do well when they seek to reduce this painful distance.

In what ways do you and your spouse view your adult son or daughter differently?

The challenge of maintaining a kindred relationship with a divorced son or daughter is difficult when a mother believes her child's irresponsible lifestyle caused a marital breakup. That's how it is with Lillian Goodrich and her forty-year-old daughter, Casey. Although the two of them had talked to each other nearly every day of Casey's twenty-year marriage, Lillian now seldom sees her daughter, who lives a stone's throw away from the Goodrich's Morgan horse and sheep ranch in central Oregon.

On a visit to their home, Lillian offered me tea as we talked about her daughter. She admitted she had never imagined Casey would even think about divorce. When it came, this devoted mother was terribly shocked by the news: "Why, I didn't *even know* there was trouble!" she begins. "We'd always been so close." But when Casey no longer phoned or dropped in to visit, Lillian suspected her daughter was having an affair. "My son-in-law told me about Casey's secret life. She was furious at him! But I would have found out sooner or later," Lillian assures me.

The Goodrich family has been deeply involved in their church all of their lives. That is, until Casey's divorce. "Casey left our congregation," Lillian says with regret. "I told her, 'I'll miss you a lot.' And I do."

The phone rings. It's Casey.

"Hello, dear," Lillian says brightly. "Yes, we're having Daniel's birthday dinner here tomorrow night. It's all arranged. The girls are helping with everything. No, Daniel doesn't know. It's a surprise.... *You bet* he'll be pleased we remembered!" Lillian continues her description of tomorrow evening's family gala. Then slowly and distinctly she says, "We'll miss you, dear. I love you," and replaces a handheld receiver on the old-fashioned wall phone.

"Oh, I pray for her," Lillian confides as she returns to the settee. "I think Casey's glad that I care so much for Daniel—that's Casey's ex-husband. I suppose my caring for him lets her off the hook, yet Casey still wants to know what her girls are doing for their dad and so on. So, I tell her. I'm just glad that she calls now and then.

"We're friends, but it's a surface friendship. I feel guarded all the time. Casey told me, 'Be careful what you say, mom.' So I have. I don't want to drive a bigger wedge between us," Lillian reflects.

Staring into a cup of tea grown cold, Lillian reminisces: "Maybe I kept Casey reined in too tightly while she was a teenager, even after she married. She and Daniel and their children lived just down the road. I knew everything that went on in their family. At least I thought I did. Now Casey doesn't want me to know *anything* about her life," she says sadly, describing the distance the divorce had wedged between them. "I bite my tongue a lot. I want her to be happy, yet I resent that she has torn this family apart," Lillian says testily.

"I cannot accept what Casey has done, what she continues to do. I do love her, but it's impossible not to have an opinion. If I blame her outright, I'll lose her. I couldn't bear that." Lillian sighs heavily.

This hurting mother just keeps praying. The previous spring she had invited Casey to go with her to a weekend women's retreat on the Oregon coast. One evening at the retreat, mother and daughter knelt and prayed together. "That gave me hope," Lillian says with misty eyes. "If Casey and I can continue to talk and to pray, I know we haven't lost everything."

REACH OUT AND TOUCH

Fragmented families in our mobile society make creative communication a must. Modern technology is filling the gap. We can conveniently keep in touch via the Internet, by fax, and by e-mail. Nearly everyone has an answering machine, and the option for visual telephone connections may soon catch on.

The telephone is probably the easiest way to "reach out and touch" across the miles. Over the phone, we come into each other's homes, hear the children laugh and the dog bark, and sense the everyday ongoing lives of our adult children and their families.

Agreeing on a consistent time to phone helps children to anticipate your call. Have at least one specific reason for calling. Sincerity (or lack of it) can be picked up, even over the telephone. Keep a diary of phone conversations, jotting down things that are important in your childrens' lives. Transfer important dates from your phone diary to your prayer list.

Keep photos handy to look at as you talk. Open-ended statements are best: "I'm interested in how your week went" or "I'm concerned about how you're feeling now" (they had the flu the last time you talked) or "When is your proficiency exam scheduled?" If they mention names of their friends, jot those down so you can ask about them occasionally too.

Your divorced child will welcome a call on his birthday and other special occasions. Particularly the first year after a divorce, remember him on what would have been his wedding anniversary. Think about what he would like to hear. Then, if you can say it sincerely, say it.

If you feel you're only a "crying shoulder" for a barrage of bitterness, ask your adult child to tell you about something *good* that's happened this week. Then reinforce the positive by telling them you are glad they had a fun time.

Do you feel connected to your adult child's life?
How often do you telephone?
Who usually initiates the contact?

If it's been a long time since your divorced son or daughter phoned, don't brood, call. Emotionally, your adult child will probably be "up" one call, "down" the next. Listen with your heart to their tone of voice. What feelings do you sense? Are they harried from an overloaded schedule and pressures at work, or frustrated with children? Acknowledge their feelings as valid ones.

When life is grim, help your divorced child clarify the facts. Help her separate thinking (rational options) from feelings (irrational options). Be compassionate, but don't deprive her of working through her own problems. Expressing concern, say, "I'm really sorry you have so many trials right now. Remember that I care about you."

If she's already made a poor decision, your saying, "We all learn," is much more affirming than, "You should have *known* better!" We all have the right to goof up our lives. Share your own experience of making it through fearful or tough times. Your vulnerability will bond you closer and perhaps open up a new level of communication.

End phone conversations with "I love you." (If you're not comfortable with the sound of those words, practice!) Love, sincerely expressed, tells your child you value her as a person and cherish her connection to the family, even as she's a pilgrim in her own life journey. Learn to give your child your blessing. Just a simple, "The Lord bless you and keep you," even over the phone, is sustaining.

Nancy and John shared with me their initial experience of keeping in touch with their newly divorced son, Kevin, who lived several states away. "Because Kevin was in deep denial we phoned nearly every day," Nancy says. "I believe it helped him heal emotionally for us to just listen."

When Kevin had an unfortunate physical encounter with his estranged wife's boyfriend, Nancy recalls Kevin's plea over the phone: "'I don't know what to do!' Since he had a broken jaw, we advised him to go to a hospital," she says, now smiling at such an obvious suggestion.

For many months, Nancy often talked with Kevin by phone until two in the morning. "I asked thousands of questions to *keep* him talking, help him ventilate and get in touch with his grief, disappointment, and anger," Nancy explains.

Nancy recalls an explosive call that came one evening. "Mom, you won't believe this one!" Kevin had stormed. "She's [the ex-wife] charged me with sexually molesting [one of his daughters]."

"Kevin was raving mad!" Nancy remembers. "I also heard hurt in his voice. He was devastated: 'Why would she do this to me?' he wailed.

"John and I tried to help Kevin move from anger to action," Nancy explains. "At first he resisted, but finally he submitted to the psychological testing his lawyer recommended, and that acquitted him." Nancy believes those charges helped jolt him into the reality of the finality of the divorce.

Through the ordeal of the divorce, Kevin's parents continued to phone him. Although Kevin had a Christian upbringing, they didn't expect him to be particularly "spiritual" during this time—and they didn't want to sound pious or impractical. With his permission, Nancy prayed with Kevin over the telephone for specific things such as the ability to work well at his job, the children's adjustment at school, a good housekeeper, someone to play tennis with—the ongoing things of life, when life had seemed to him to cease.

At the end of the settlement, Kevin had custody of all four children. So the calls continue, now multiplied, as Nancy and John spend long-distance time with their grandchildren too.

"Our hearts were broken through this divorce," Nancy says. "But John and I pledged to pray together, not just wring our hands in worry. We're proud of how Kevin's come through this. He's the best 'Mr. Mom' there is anywhere!"

WRITE OFTEN

When you have something serious to say, writing may be a better choice than a phone call. Letters are tangible and can be read—and reread—for clarification and for comfort. These letters become keepsakes, valid proof of parental care and concern. So, write; you can always talk about it later.

In letters, encourage your adult child to share with you his professional dreams, educational desires, plans to keep in shape physically, intent to get counseling, and resolve to grow spiritually. Without making judgments, promise to pray for these goals. You'll have some significant things to inquire about as you continue to write and call.

Maybe your lonely daughter is considering adopting a child as a single parent. "What do you think about it?" she writes to ask. If you and your spouse cannot agree on such an issue, simply say it's been impossible for you to come to a joint conclusion. Don't make an issue of your differences: "Well, I think ... but your dad thinks. ..." Your hurting adult needs you, as parents, to be whole. Belaboring your division will only heighten her hurt.

Two of Joleen Johnson's adult daughters are both recently divorced. One marriage had lasted seven years, the other twenty-three. Since they live some distance away, Joleen recalls calling and writing often. Her long letters were cathartic, especially for her daughter Martie, who had decided to leave an abusive relationship. "Our respect conveyed confidence and, I hope, made her choices easier," Joleen said.

For their younger daughter, Erin, the Johnsons' tactic was different. Joleen and her husband Al felt that Erin's lifestyle had precipitated the marriage breakup. "We were honest," Joleen said. "We wrote and told Erin we were not happy with her lifestyle, and told her why. When she and her live-in boyfriend asked to visit us, we suggested they stay at a local motel. Al and I candidly told them our choice was to not invite them to our home overnight."

If you have trouble discussing sensitive issues with your divorced child, try composing a letter explaining your viewpoint. Read it over as you think your son or daughter would. How will he or she accept this message from you?

Your letters to a divorced adult about important issues may never be answered, but they will not go unread. Be careful in committing yourself in print, however. After writing about a sensitive subject, put the letter away unmailed. In several days, get out the letter and read it over. Ask your spouse or a trusted friend to read it and evaluate the "tone" of the letter. If it rings true *and* it needs to be said, mail it.

PERSONAL VISITS

Traditional-minded parents idealize holidays as prime family time. But your children have their own responsibilities and interests now. Planning for "Christmas in July" may be more practical.

Getting adult children together to celebrate the holidays is difficult when they are single. Consider how the mother in the following role-play might have found a mutually agreeable plan for her adult child's visit. Whether you are videotaping or reading in your group, let several different people take turns playing the parts.

Cast: Mother in Denver, adult child (man or woman) in Philadelphia

Scene: Telephone conversation, split stage

Mother: We're going to have the biggest family Christmas ever! I've got the whole week planned for everyone. We'll get your ticket to fly in on Friday evening, December 21. I'll bet you're so excited you can't wait!

Child: Well, I'm not sure I can get away for that long.

Mother: What do you mean, you can't get away? I checked your school schedule. You're out on Friday. You can come.

Child: Mom, I've really been looking forward to a little vacation this year. My teaching load is so full, I need a break.

Mother: Sure you do, dear. That's why I'm planning to spend so much to make you happy. All your aunts and uncles and cousins are coming. Your dad and I are not so young any more, you know. This could be our last big family holiday. You never know.

Child: I didn't know that you and Dad haven't been well. I'd really feel bad if I let you down. But, well, you see, I signed up for a ski trip with a divorce recovery group from my church and I was looking forward to going. It's just for three days. I could still be there for Christmas Day.

Mother: I can't believe that you'd rather be out in the cold wind with a group of strangers instead of with your very own family. We've always been together. What would I tell people? No, dear. I expect you to be on that plane on the twenty-first. No more excuses.

Child: Really, Mom, I'm not making excuses. I want to go skiing with my friends.

Mother: If you go skiing, don't expect to come dragging in here midweek. After all we've done for you, the least you could do is to come home a week at Christmas. You know, some day you won't have us anymore. Your sister and brother don't let us down. We're thinking of revising our will, and we'll remember how you treat your parents.

Adult: Of course I'll be there, Mom. I'll be on that plane on Friday, the twenty-first. I want to make you happy.

Are your expectations for family holiday celebrations always realistic? Take a poll of your adult children to find out how they feel about family get-togethers.

Although parents are more likely to want their children to come "home" to visit, you'll learn more by visiting them on their own turf. If you have the time and finances, go—if you're invited. If you hint that you'd like to come, be willing to accept their response either way.

Arrange ahead of time where you'll stay. A motel might be worth the freedom for both of you. A few days' visit is usually more welcome than a weeklong stay. If you both want to spend more time together, go to a neutral place—a conference ground, tent camping, or a resort. The more activities you can share, the more likely your divorced child will look forward to your visits.

What are some activities that you and your divorced child mutually enjoy? How can you incorporate one or more of these activities into your next visit?

If your visits seem to disintegrate day by day, take notes on what causes the spiral. Maybe certain issues ought to be avoided. Let your adult child know you're willing to put those aside. And when you visit, keep some personal space, flexibility, and choice.

Some parents complain that they have nothing to talk about with their adult child. If that's the case for you, find things to talk about. Clip and send news stories and ask his opinion about current events. Even if you always initiate the calls, write the letters, and go visit, don't give up! Your son is thinking mostly about himself and his own needs. If your love hinges on receiving, you'll be disappointed.

Geographical distance need not affect your bond with a divorced son or daughter. Your greatest influence is not through physical proximity but through emotional and spiritual closeness. Convey confidence in him, and in the process give him the freedom to express the whole range of human experience while you enfold him in a warm and wide family hug.

5

COPING WITH SINGLES BACK HOME AGAIN

Directions to Angelica's home on an American Indian Reservation in Arizona were sketchy: "One-quarter mile beyond the crossroads, in a row of houses with an ugly fence," she had said on the phone. The flat land is framed by an early November sunset. Dotted with spectral yucca plants and eerie rock formations, the terrain looks more like a moonscape than a hamlet for hundreds of Native American families.

Everyone seems to know everyone on the reservation, and they point me down this road and that one. I finally pull alongside my destination—the homes of four generations of women ranging in age from five to seventy-five.

I turn off the ignition and spot Angelica in her front yard, a ruddy-skinned, rotund, matronly woman, wearing an apron seldom removed. As we sit and talk in the evening alpenglow, Angelica claims that her family is so big she "can't count 'em all," at least not her grandchildren. Her dark eyes dance with love as she talks about her eight living children and a stepchild, all with families of their own. Her oldest daughter, Sapphire, lives in the adjoining house, and Sapphire's daughter and her two young daughters live in a nearby trailer.

"Children want to get away . . . then they want to come home," Angelica says with a wry smile. Unpretentiously she pulls braided hair to her plump chest and methodically untangles the plaits as she continues: "Through the years, I mostly raised my children by myself, and helped raise a lot of their children too. At one time I had three families back home." Angelica brushes her flowing white hair as she talks.

What caused the families to break apart? "Too much drinking," Angelica says without hesitation. "There's too much violence now for young people to grow up in." Swift strokes of the brush punctuate her strong words.

Sapphire, who works in a community health office, arrives home and joins us in the cool desert twilight. Unobtrusively she stands aside, gripping a mesh shopping bag as if she were going on by, but continues to listen intently to our conversation. Abruptly, she joins in: "Yes, too much violence!" Her black eyes flash as she nods her head.

Sapphire then recalls her own stormy teenage years, when she had been abused by an alcoholic father, Angelica's first husband. "My dad kicked me out when I was fifteen. I bragged that I'd never get married, but I wanted kids. I had one child before I was married; when my marriage broke up, I was pregnant with my third."

A sturdy woman now in her mid-fifties, Sapphire has come back home off and on through the years. After Sapphire's divorce, Angelica built a small brick house next door for herself and gave the original adobe to her oldest daughter.

"If someone asks me if a parent should let children come home, I'd say no. But that's exactly what I did," Angelica says sheepishly through a candid, near-toothless grin.

Author Stephen Bly says there are four things a parent needs to do before saying no: listen, think, discuss, and pray.

About prayer he says, "There is higher knowledge. There is divine wisdom. There's a response that will work for the eternal good of all parties involved. But you'll never find it unless you take time to talk to God."[1] Angelica, like pliant parents in every culture, finds it hard to say no to her children at any stage of their life. But home-again adult children and their parents both need to learn to cope with the choices they make.

WHAT WILL BE THE CONSEQUENCES?

Mom is in her mid-fifties; Dad, sixty, just took an early retirement. They've launched dreams for recreation and travel. No children have lived at home for nearly ten years now. Daughter Sidney was the last to be married, to a man she met on vacation in Puerto Vallarta. Now she's divorced. And Sidney's been so despondent! Her parents pray, but they also worry. How has she made it through another week!?

The phone rings. It's Sidney. Mom is relieved to hear from her, yet distressed to know she's really "down." She listens to a litany of problems: house payments, broken-down car, distress with her job, depression, loneliness. "How can we help?" Mom asks sincerely. Sidney's unexpected response: "Can I come home?"

How can you build a solid relationship with your adult children before they find they need to move back home with you?

Before you say yes to your adult child's request to come back home, consider the precedent you will be setting. If you have several grown children, can you open your home to one and later refuse another? If you say yes to your divorced child, it's crucial that you have your eyes open. Adults may look on coming "home" to their parents as their birthright—a haven in a heartless world. But remember, your "kid" is not coming home; you'll be hosting a resident-guest who happens to have a birth relationship.

Robert Frost called home the place where, when you go there, they have to take you in. But parents of divorced adults are not obligated to say yes. Parents might very well reject an adult child's request because of habits or behavior incompatible with their own lifestyle.

If there are minor children at home, the parents' first obligation is to honor the rights and territory of the younger children. These children need to feel connected rather than displaced by an older brother or sister. Explain the status differences in responsibilities (paying rent) and freedoms (no curfew). If your adult child will be coming back home because of emotional difficulties, explain the problem in terms the younger child can understand. Secrets only keep family members apart.

Invite (or allow) your divorced child to come home to live for awhile because you sincerely want to help, not because you'd feel guilty saying no. Look carefully at your priorities. Know what God has called you to do at this time in your life. Your call may not be compatible with taking in a divorced family.

When the Chan's divorced daughter and her two children moved home, the Chans found that they needed to model a lot of "tough love." Peter and Ruth, both in their sixties, are typical family-minded Orientals. After Laurie's divorce, they wanted to be part of the answer to her problems, so they moved to a larger house where everyone could have more privacy. Ruth took charge of her grandchildren while Laurie returned to school.

The scene was set for two families, but it seemed as if the actors had different scripts. Not slipping back into old patterns of parent/child relationships was the hardest struggle for the Chans, as it is in many two-generation homes.

The Chans knew that Laurie didn't want a "free ride," so they established some structure. Ruth made weekday dinners; Laurie was to cook on weekends. Laurie would take care of her rooms and laundry and pay a small amount of rent. An important rule: After about 6:00 P.M. on weekdays, and all weekend, the children were in Laurie's care. "We needed those breaks," Ruth states.

Looking back, Peter and Ruth advise parents to help divorced families maintain separate living quarters, if at all possible. "When everyone is under the same roof, it can be explosive," Peter cautions. "Even if people don't blow up at one another, there's still an inner struggle."

Jerry and Mary White, authors of *When Your Kids Aren't Kids Anymore*, offer parental guidelines for returning adult children:

- Before the move, talk frankly about expectations.
- Put financial arrangements in writing.
- Discuss and agree on household responsibilities.
- Consider the effect on younger siblings.
- Plan some privacy for both you and your adult child.
- Agree on care and supervision of grandchildren.
- Remember, it's your home; you set the standards and spiritual tone.[2]

Building a satisfying relationship with a living-in single takes planning, mutual understanding, and wisdom. If you decide to take your divorced son or daughter in, tentatively agree on the length of their stay and a savings plan for their own place. Determine whether they will pay or barter for food and utilities. (Remember, they are neither servants nor children.) And decide how to handle your adult child's dating again— before it happens!

CONSIDER YOUR RELATIONSHIP

Having young people around again is tiring, but it's also stimulating and can keep you young at heart. You may get to know your daughter or son in a way you never could when they were teenagers.

Tom feels he's enjoying his grown daughter more because he doesn't have to be the "heavyweight"; they can relate more as adults. That doesn't mean they always have the same values, he points out. Sometimes he tells her, "I'll have to disagree," and then they go on.

If you and your spouse now live alone, picture adding your grown-up divorced single as a temporary resident. What would you enjoy or not enjoy about the arrangement?

Psychologist and speaker Jim Conway cautions, however, against inviting home an adult child with whom you have a poor or weak relationship. There will only be a "tolerant truce ... The [grown] child feels no connection with parents, but has to be there; the parents feel no connection with the [grown] child, but feel obligated. In short, the parents feel used and the younger person feels controlled."[3]

Parents may vacillate between several destructive roles when a single-again child moves home. There's the *victim* mentality: "After all I've done for you ..."; the *persecutor* role: "You made your bed, now lie on it"; the *dictator's* throne: "Under my roof you'll do what I say, or else!"; and the *rescuer* line of thought: "Come to mama. I'll make it all better."

And, as far as the adult children are concerned, going home again may be like Rip Van Winkle awakening. The territory's changed; they've changed too. In dual-family living everyone needs to adjust to new terrain. Such was the case at the Helix home.

Claire and Bill Helix's charming bed and breakfast in Arizona nestles against mysterious mountains that, from dawn to sunset, reflect serene pastel hues. The Helixes had just gotten a good start with their business when their daughter Candice returned home with a two-year-old son.

After serving a southwestern omelet breakfast, this couple told me their story: Candice was pregnant when she got married. The Helixes had encouraged the wedding because they feared Candice might otherwise choose an abortion. They bought the couple a travel trailer as a wedding gift, and Candice and her husband moved to another state.

When little Brent was almost a year old, Candice brought him to his grandparents for a brief visit. While they were there, Candice's husband phoned to say he was leaving the family.

Despite the bustling schedule of a bed and breakfast, Candice, along with baby Brent, moved in with her parents. From the beginning, Claire and Bill felt at loss to help her. "She was a child with a child," Claire says. "And she was so moody. We suspected she was still using drugs as she had as a teenager."

"Candice's temper tantrums and our business were not compatible," Bill explains. "We could see it wasn't working out." Finally, Candice began a twelve-step therapy program. The Helixes helped her apply for welfare and food stamps and moved her and Brent to a mobile home on their large ranch. Candice now cleans the guest rooms as barter for her rent, has a waitressing job, and sells her own handcrafts at a local boutique.

"We always felt she had artistic talent, if only she'd not been so rebellious. But now there's a ray of hope," Claire says with a sigh of relief.

ESTABLISH SOME HOME RULES

When divorced adults move home, proceed with caution. Some capable adult children find mom and dad's place too comfortable. Your home may be a safety net, but it shouldn't be a hammock. Make some conditions. If you don't, you'll give the negative message: "You're not capable of being responsible— you're still a child." Establish a new relationship; the old parent- teenager one won't work.

Tom and Sally found it hard to establish house rules when their single daughter arrived from another state with her two teenagers. "The children hadn't been disciplined much," Sally said. "They didn't like our rules—any rules! Although we didn't set many expectations for our adult daughter, we sure did for her kids!"

"But we rewarded them, too," added Tom, a veteran school principal. "During that year, we hosted dances on the patio and slumber parties, and encouraged our grandchildren to make friends and begin new activities. We really tried, I think."

Covenant agreements are best when written out during negotiations. By mutual agreement, changes in the contract can be made at any time. Be careful, though. If there are loopholes in the rules, your adult child will probably slide through. Maybe her dog becomes your job to feed. Or her dirty dishes in the sink greet you every morning. If you ignore offenses, your anger will fester and infect the relationship. Before your warm welcome turns into an eviction notice, consider some preventive measures.

KEEP COMMUNICATION OPEN

Don't expect a resident adult child to pick up on casual hints to talk about something that's bothering you. Instead, schedule a time to sit down and discuss the specific issue. You have a right to speak up about things that directly concern you or minor children in your home, but when you confront him or her, keep an open mind and look for positives. "I'm glad you find music a way to relax after work," you might begin before you ask that the volume be set at a level comfortable for you.

When you meet, plan to communicate and compromise. Rather than standing eyeball to eyeball, sit together; side by side, shoulder to shoulder, you can turn a possible conflict into a confabulation. Even if your opinions are rejected, your relationship will remain if you affirm being equals!

This is the time to listen to your adult child's anxieties and fears and to admit your own. Discuss job hunting, vacations, household chores, phone use, late-night noise, acceptable videos in the family room, and other bothersome matters. Really listen!

You'll find scant adult-to-adult response if you come on as the expert. "Talking down" to another adult is like patting a child on the head: a condescending gesture. However, if you agree only outwardly, the problem will likely reappear. Remember the age-old way to divide a piece of cake? One cuts, and one chooses. One of you might suggest two solutions, the other choose one. You want to create a balance in your home: a place of independence where your child feels free and comfortable, and a place of dependence where she must conform to some expectations.

What mutual responsibilities can you suggest for dual-family living?

When you're too stressed or too tired, old patterns will emerge. Stop. Apologize if necessary. Take a break: "I'm feeling uncomfortable with the discussion right now. Let's make some popcorn and talk about this again in about fifteen minutes." You'll do better with a fresh start. Love is blocked when communication breaks down. Foiled energy turns to resentment and hostility.

Few of us can be sure about exact words spoken last week, let alone last month. But we're sure about the *feelings* we had then. What is the tone of talk in your home? Is it nonjudgmental and affirming? What about your adult child's tone? If it is hostile and vindictive, call a halt: "I will not tolerate verbal abuse. When we can discuss the subject calmly, I'm ready."

In tense moments, allow time to get your emotions under control. Then when you do comment, say, "I feel . . . I think . . . I would like." Be direct. For example, "I want our home smoke free. I believe smoke is unhealthy and I really don't like the smell." Find nonjudgmental ways to state your opinions. Avoid "you should," which is quickly translated into, "I'm wrong . . . I'm bad."

Ask your spouse to check to see how often you use the terms "good-bad, right-wrong." Words are powerful. They pierce, wound, and infect; they also soothe, heal, and build. Writer and speaker Tim Stafford coined the term "toxic talk" for harsh words and shaded truth. "Toxic talk is poisonous," he says. "It estranges people . . . and whole families." For an antidote, Stafford suggests examining all conversation in a very systematic way, recording each interaction in a notebook, to see what causes toxicity and what needs to be changed. "When you do an inventory of your words, the careless words stare you in the face," says Stafford.[4]

So monitor your mouth. Moderate your tone. Your voice meter is in your brain; your thoughts precede your words. Make your thoughts prayer thoughts. And when you're ready, speak gracefully.

Before discussing a routine difference with your resident divorced child, jot down words that probably describe his feelings. Knowing this, how might you adjust your approach?

Open communication is supposed to reveal points of conflict. In fact, if you live together and don't have some disagreements, you're probably not communicating very deeply. Allow conflict. Encourage it. Resolving it can help you and your adult children to be closer than ever before.

The parents and their divorced daughter in the following skit have several unresolved conflicts. As you read, think about whether you identify with the choleric mom or the phlegmatic dad.

Cast: Parents Harry and Lenore, divorced daughter Karla, Karla's friend Betsy

Scenes: Stage right: Harry and Lenore, having coffee at home. Stage left: Karla and Betsy, having coffee in an office lounge.

Lenore: Do you know what time Karla came home last night? I'll tell you! 2:30 A.M., that's when! How does she expect to be any good for anything today? Oh, I wish she would grow up!

Harry: Now, Mom, don't get so flustered. Maybe she'll go to bed early tonight, or fall asleep watching TV.

Lenore: Yeah! While I'm slaving away in the kitchen doing *her* dishes!

Karla: You're lucky not to live at home, Betsy.

Betsy: Yeah? . . . Why? Seems to me like it would be pretty soft living.

Karla: No way! I feel like my mom is watching every move I make. Last night she left a laundry basket full of my clothes where I had to trip over them at 2 A.M. At dinner she's always telling me what I should or shouldn't eat.

Lenore: Looks like I'm headed to the grocery store—again. Karla is eating us out of house and home. She really packs the food away on weekends. Harry, let's start charging her more for board. She's a working woman!

Harry: Now, honey, sometimes she isn't home at all. Are you gonna credit her for *not* eating? Just let it go.

Lenore: Well, I'll let it go a little longer. But *only* a little longer. One of these days I'm gonna just up and tell her to move on. I'm getting tired of being housekeeper, cook, and baker.

Karla: I'd like to tell my folks that I'm ready to move out. But I think they really like having me around.

Betsy: Hey, I'm going to lose my housemate next month. Why don't you come live with me? We could share a ride to work too. It'd be great!

Karla: You know, maybe I will. At least I'll seriously think about it. I sure don't want to hurt my folks' feelings, though. They've been really good to me since my divorce last year. Despite Mom's being so bossy and nosy, I do love them both.

After reading the role-play, discuss Karla and her parents'
differing views. What would make things go more smoothly in
this home?

PROCEED WITH CAUTION

A divorced adult child can add an overwhelming emotional and financial burden to the life of a middle-aged woman
who is also single. Mary Ellen, a single woman in Nashville,
begged her daughter Lynette to come home after Lynette's dev-
astating and unexpected divorce. She found it difficult to accept
when her single daughter said, "Mom, I've been gone over five
years. I think it would be too hard on us both." Instead, Lynette
moved close by; Mary Ellen now admits that this was probably best after all.

Corwin and Margaret Freeman's twice-divorced daughter came home only occasionally, when she was too sick to
work. When she was home she would revert to being "the
child," and neither she nor her parents liked the resulting
upheaval. "If children can be independent, they need to be,"
Corwin says. "When they come home, it drains parents of time,
energy, and money. I know we just kept giving to the last drop."

Inviting children home may be more of a fantasy than a
working reality. Divorced adults who come home to a turned-
down bed may find that they don't fit as well in the nest as they
once did. They and you are at different stages of life. If your single comes for a short time and then announces his wish to move
on, be positive. Appreciate his need for independence. Be glad
that your home could be a "watering hole" to refresh him on his
way. And most of all, assure him that your prayers and loving
support are with him wherever he goes.

6

DEALING WITH SEX, SUBSTANCE ABUSE, AND MONEY

Parents harp about their adult child's weight, dress, hairstyle, use of time, choice of friends, college attendance, getting ahead, and sexual standards. The differences widen when there is also a gap in religious views.

One mom says that talking to her headstrong son about his lifestyle is like "driving with my foot on the brake." She wants to say, "Stop! Stop thinking like that!" Her body tenses and her mind melts as she struggles to shift into neutral when talking with him.

Parents of a divorced son or daughter who tended in the past to ignore the variant lifestyle of their married offspring may find that lifestyle harder to avoid when their single moves back home again or when their financial help is needed. George Gallup Jr. cites a recent poll that shows that the values of eighteen- to twenty-nine-year-olds differ greatly from those of people over fifty. "Marked differences exist about premarital sex, abortion, equal rights, legalizing homosexuality, self-expression, marijuana use, work, and authority," Gallup says.[1] Because of our rapidly changing mores, the gap between the view of these two age groups is likely to widen.

Lillian is piqued at the antics of her divorced forty-year-old daughter. "Casey acts like a teenager! I'm embarrassed to be around her," Lillian blurts. Other parents express frustration about the Generation X attitude of "get in, get out, and leave the debris." They disdain their adult children's hang-loose attitude about everything from easy-come-easy-go job transitions to uncommitted relationships. Some parents wonder if their children's reticence for real commitments—including lifetime marriage—is affected by our unstable, fast-paced culture.

Seeing life from your adult child's perspective is not the same as liking his choices. He still needs to know you love him despite your differences in worldviews. Even if you're bewildered by your divorced son's life choices that profoundly violate your own values, commit to walk beside him. Express your concern for his tough job of coping in a turbulent time. Ultimately, we love people, not lifestyles.

Parents can disagree without being disagreeable. It's important for you to be consistent. Generational differences can be tolerated more readily by

- analyzing our own experiences (be honest) at a similar age or stage in life;
- analyzing the ways our parents interacted with us;
- asking God to give us compassion.

Tempestuous issues bring on three treacherous emotions—fear, guilt, and shame—according to John White, former professor of psychiatry at the University of Manitoba. If these emotions conquer us, we're lost. "But if we [parents] conquer [these emotions], our experience will be turned to our profit."[2]

While not excusing immoral behavior, parents need to understand the world from their adult child's perspective. Some issues are obviously more perilous than others. Let's sort out the serious ones.

SEXUALITY

Upon discovering that your divorced adult child is living with someone before remarriage, or even cohabiting with someone of the same sex, perhaps one tack for mid-generation parents is to be more curious and less reactive. Concern and curiosity will keep the door of communication open better than condemnation will.

When you feel strongly that a certain lifestyle is wrong, be prepared with accurate medical facts, not just fear-filled thoughts. Read, talk with your spouse, and pray about your concerns. Note quotes from credible Christian authors and jot down key Scriptures. It's an important "plumb line" for parents to say, with good reasons to back them up, what they think about sexual relationships. Once said, the message need not be repeated.

Another pointer: Give your opinion, not an ultimatum about your adult child's lifestyle choices. The more you say "You're wrong," the more she's likely to try to prove she's right. Criticism is like a quagmire, bogging down rather than building up relationships. This skit may launch a lively discussion in your group.

In the following role-play, analyze whether parents Edna and Clyde are able to keep their good intentions for family bonds when their divorced daughter throws them a curve.

Cast: Father, Clyde; mother, Edna; and daughter, Darbi, a twenty-five-year-old divorcée

Scene: Clyde and Edna's living room, sometime after midnight

Clyde: 'Bout time you're home! I suppose you've been at that wicked man's apartment again. I don't want to know doing what!

Edna: Clyde, remember we agreed we wouldn't let differences destroy our family. *(Turning to Darbi)* Honey, we're really concerned about you. Your lifestyle is tearing us apart. But even though we don't like how you're living, we still love you.

Clyde: What she needs to do is go take a cold shower! Snap out of it, Darbi. Get rid of that bum!

Darbi: When do I get to say something? You're always harping about how I run my life—my skirts are too short, my friends are no good. You keep bringing up that I never finished college, that I don't go to church, and other things that are *your* values, not mine.

Clyde: Let me tell you something about values, young lady. Here's what Scripture says about a loose woman: "Her feet go down to death; her steps lead straight to the grave."

Darbi: Don't spout Scripture at me. I just don't buy it! Maybe you do, but I don't.

Edna: I'm sure you have reasons for feeling that way, dear. It's just that we've found that the Bible has helped us deal with problems. We think it could help you too.

Darbi: I'm moving in with Lance tomorrow. If I choose to live with him, I'd rather do it openly.

Clyde: Good riddance! Just don't let him come around here when I'm home!

Edna: I don't really understand all the feelings you have to cope with right now, Darbi. I wish I did. I know there's nothing wrong in having sensual desires. And I also know that sexual ideas begin in the mind before the body. It will take time for you to adjust to being single again. We'd like to see you heal emotionally before getting involved so quickly. What would help you put your passionate feelings in perspective right now?

Clyde: Humph! Let's just agree to disagree!

Darbi: Well, Lance pressures me more when he's been drinking. That does trouble me.

Clyde: I knew it! That good-for-nothin'!

Edna: Hush, Clyde. *(Turning to her daughter)* Darbi, your dad and I want the best for you because we love you. God

> wants the best for you too, honey. I'm asking him to help you every day. Please, won't you reconsider your thoughts about living with Lance?

Darbi: Let me sleep on it. Whatever I do, I love you both. Goodnight now.

What were the family interactions in the role-play? Edna and Clyde had agreed to keep the family bonds; how did Clyde "blow it"? Describe Edna's reactions. Is Darbi honest about her feelings? What might help Darbi discover God's love and the direction of the Holy Spirit? What do you think will happen the next day?

If you had difficulty talking about sexual matters with your son or daughter as they grew up, you probably still have difficulty bringing up the subject. But if you have a good adult-adult relationship, you don't have to steer away from all conversation about sex. Certainly you can remark that it's difficult to be single without a sexual partner. Or that the creative forces of love can be fulfilled in many ways of selfless giving. Do you have experience to offer from your own life? Share that.

You may also share that Christians don't have to deny their desires by suppressing them. If they allow, the Holy Spirit can give a new set of acceptable desires that brings emotional and physical fulfillment. Says author Tim Stafford: "The Spirit provides self-control . . . a quality that grows naturally out of life in the Spirit." But, says Stafford, "Life in the Spirit is not religious cruise control. Life in the Spirit is warfare. It takes all that your mind and body have to give."[3]

Historically, Christians who follow God's Word have given high status to celibacy. "Celibacy is, like marriage, a sign of the Kingdom," Stafford says. "Celibacy can be lived with grace and joy."[4] In this faithful commitment, Christ offers single people a special inner joy.

Although your divorced adult may be in her thirties, she will be thrust back into some things she went through as a teenager. Will nice men want to date her? Can she handle the rejection of not being asked out at all for weeks on end? Can she be a friend to a man without assumptions being made? Can she handle the sexual temptations of the singles' scene? With the prevalence of AIDS, there are both medical and moral considerations to her choices.

It's difficult to be alone at any phase of life. Tell your adult child that you're trusting God for wholesome new friendships for him or her. Meanwhile, you can heal the hurt somewhat. Real love is generic. When love fills your family circle, your divorced adult may have less need to frantically search for it elsewhere.

SUBSTANCE ABUSE

Joleen Johnson, whose three out of four children are divorced, believes that today's cultural influences hit the family hard. "Divorce is not God's plan for marriage, but neither is dependency on alcohol and drugs," she says.

The lovely country club where we agreed to meet for lunch was an unlikely backdrop for the agonizing story Joleen shared with me about her daughter Martie's life being nearly emotionally destroyed by divorce.

Martie's husband was heavily into drugs and refused rehabilitation. Joleen and her husband saw no other way out and encouraged Martie to get her own apartment. As if it wasn't enough for substance abuse to destroy Martie's marriage, her teenage children became drug users and chose to live with their father.

Worry over her children threw Martie into deep depression. "Martie wore only black and sat curled up in a ball. Her self-esteem was nil," Joleen said, staring into space as if she were seeing a rerun of those days.

Each time Martie was hospitalized, Joleen and her husband rushed to catch the next cross-country flight. "We'd go and just be there," says Joleen. "I'd point out the positive and tell Martie she had been a good mother."

A leave of absence from her job allowed Martie to come to her parents' home for a few weeks. Joleen recalled those difficult days: "First we took long walks, later on she was able to shop some, watch funny videos, or just talk."

Finally, Joleen and her husband helped Martie buy furniture for her own apartment near where her children lived. Martie had gone to work part-time and seemed to be getting her footing when her counselor was killed in a plane crash. Joleen remembered Martie's stormy phone call to her parents: "How could God take away my lifeline—my best friend?"

"Do you want us to come?" they had asked.

Because the Johnsons were willing to ask and accept the answer either way, Martie was comforted by just knowing her parents *would* come. When Martie answered, "No, I'll make it if I can call you when I need to," Joleen and her husband knew their daughter was healing.

During Martie's crisis, the Johnsons developed stronger family ties than ever before. The trust relationship with her parents is helping Martie return to a healthy, stable life.

Can you separate your positive feelings for your divorced child as a person from his/her compulsive negative habits? Can you model God's love? See 1 John 4:7–8.

If you suspect your adult child is using harmful and addictive drugs, the sooner you get the problem out in the open, the better. If your adult child lives in your home, you can insist on a periodic urinalysis. Only after everyone admits there's a problem and cooperates in getting help will change occur.

Substance abuse is a serious issue with ramifications for the entire family. Because it's a way for the user to ignore emotional needs, good counseling is imperative—not only for the abuser but also for those close to him. Parents and other concerned family members might begin with Al-Anon, a support group designed to help find ways to cope with compulsive drinking in the family. (See the resource section at the back of this book.)

In a lighter vein, be understanding about casual lifestyle choices if they are different from your own. For example, if your healthy son occasionally prefers beer with his meal and you are opposed to alcohol in any form, try to accept rather than analyze his choice. Order yourself a Coke without comment and join in conversation about things that keep your relationship warm and friendly.

MONEY

Most divorced adults have money problems. Bailing out your divorced child certainly changes the picture drastically, but is it always wise? Lending and borrowing money is a touchy subject. When your adult child approaches you for money you have a right to ask hard questions. Giving money ought to be well thought out except in a rare crisis. Learn how to separate your adult child's need from his greed. A good first response is, "Let me consider that for a few days." You've listened, and you've reserved the right to ponder and pray.

When the time comes to give an answer, it's less than helpful to be wishy-washy. Be clear, not wordy with overlapping excuses. If you can, give your adult child two options acceptable to you and let him choose. This gives him an element of control, respects his rights, and keeps him responsible for the conditions.

Under what conditions should you consider a loan to your adult children rather than a gift of money?

Financial help carries overtones unlike any other aspect of a parent/adult child relationship. Giving carries expectations and can have long-term reverberations. As a parent you wonder how the money will be spent, even if you have suggested conditions. Meanwhile, your adult child wonders whether there's more to come and whether the financial help ought to be repaid.

And what about other adult children in your family who are still married? Siblings may scream, "Not fair!" when you assist a needy divorced brother or sister. Do you feel you must do something of equal cost for them? If you give a large amount to one child, you'll spread thin the amount left to help others, and that needs explanation as well.

Without a definitive answer to the dilemma, I offer this: give freely or not at all. However, it's not wise to put your own care in jeopardy. The linchpin seems to be good communication in order to prevent resentment or unreasonable expectations. If you feel "put upon," or if you rescue before being asked to help, your giving is apt to backfire. And saying, "I never had anyone give *me* anything . . . you've got it easy," spoils the pot. The Bible directs us well: "Each man should give what he has decided in his heart to give, not reluctantly or under compulsion, for God loves a cheerful giver" (2 Cor. 9:7).

What choices have other parents made about gifts and loans? Perhaps you agree with Irene's attitude toward her divorced daughter, Monica: "As long as I have a dime, she gets a nickel." Or are you apt to do what Mary Ellen does—slip her divorced daughter fifty dollars now and then? "Lynette never asks for it," says Mary Ellen, "but she always thanks me."

The Helix family in Arizona supplements Candice's utilities and medical bills. "I don't even want to know how much!" exclaims Claire Helix, whose husband writes the checks. Andrea and Orion in Atlanta helped daughter Leah reestablish her catering business. "We wanted to do things to help her help herself," the couple explain.

Some say that an anonymous gift is the most meaningful. "When I pay a bill for my son without his knowledge he feels that somebody cares and he must be worth their caring," one parent said. "I like that, instead of his being subjected to me and my pocketbook."

The Schallers, who have multiple divorces in their family, set limits to their giving. "No bailing out of jail or other jams," says Walter. "We can't justify using retirement money when our abusive kids expect handouts. That's wrong. Parents who give up their savings have nothing left."

Lydia and Gaylord helped divorced Lisa set up a new apartment. They felt that nice furniture would give her a fresh start and restore her self-worth. And Randall Campbell, in D.C., who wouldn't spend "just to please" his daughter, did provide a secure place for Shana to live. A tip: If you loan money to your divorced child to buy a home in his or her name, agree in writing that your loan will be repaid if and when the house is sold. This protects your investment from being used in other ways, or lost in yet another divorce settlement down the line.

The cost of education is often cited by parents as a worthwhile investment in a divorced adult's life, as is paying for counseling. The Johnsons send a monthly check for their single daughter's job training. "At first Martie wasn't comfortable accepting our help," Joleen says. "Now she knows it's the only way she can keep going."

Another drain on a divorced child's finances is attorney fees. Parents might help here. Legal agreements are necessary in every divorce, whether or not children are involved. Courts cannot legislate equality and fairness, but a good attorney may keep your single adult from becoming a battered and bruised statistic.

Some couples told me their single-parent son or daughter would not ask for *any* help, even when their refrigerator was empty. It's a mistake to manipulate a proud person into asking for help. Simply bring basic foods for their pantry. Their guilt in not being able to provide for their family may keep them from overt appreciation, but if they accept your low-key gift, you'll know they're grateful.

Parents want their adult child to love them. But money does not secure that love. Money is a means to an end, not an end in itself. Wayne and Tracy, who had repeatedly rescued

their divorced daughter from self-inflicted financial predicaments, saw money become an unhealthy symbol for their love.
"If you really cared about me, you'd . . ." was the wail from Tara,
their somewhat selfish daughter, before her parents decided
to tighten their purse strings.

"As parents we unwittingly acted out expected roles,"
states Wayne. "We finally saw that our 'help' was causing Tara
to continue to depend on us. Since we have two other grown
children with needs of their own, we decided to distribute our
resources more equitably and hold firm. When we changed our
script, Tara had to change hers."

When you need to hang tough, family counselor Arthur
Maslow suggests a quasi-legal document signed by both parents and their adult child. It notes that after a certain date the
parents will no longer honor their adult child's debts, and that
the son or daughter agrees to be responsible for living on their
own salary. The document ends with the hope that "we shall set
[name of adult child] free, not ever from our love, but from our
keeping."[5]

*What if your single son does not meet his
responsibility for child support? Should you?*

What most adult children want from their parents is not
money, but trust and love. A secure place in the family gives
them the strength to face financial issues, as well as other life
problems, including recovery from divorce. Said Ruth Chan: "It
may be easier to send money, but risking closeness takes more
courage."

SETTING BOUNDARIES

"Do you know why Mommy punished you?" you may
remember asking your youngster when you were a first-decade
parent. "Because you don't love me," was the likely reply. It
takes maturity to realize that parents correct out of love rather

than malice. When a distraught divorced child struggles with parental rejection to her requests she may again cry, "You don't love me!"

As a parent, "trying harder" doesn't do the job; being too soft with adult children doesn't work. Taking responsibility for an adult child's life is, in fact, disastrous to his growth and stability. When an adult child expects you to do things you're not comfortable with—telling his boss he's sick when he's not, doing his research paper for a graduate class, paying for a speeding ticket, or loaning him thousands of dollars—hang tough. He'll mature by facing self-made predicaments. Pawning his difficulties off on you just hinders his progress.

A book and video by the authors and clinical psychologists Henry Cloud and John Townsend suggest that the answer is *boundaries:* "A boundary is a property line. It defines where you begin and end. . . . Your boundaries define you in relation to others."[6] Boundaries demand honesty—honesty about parental wishes to control our adult children instead of controlling our own behavior.

Healthy boundaries both protect and form a comfortable pattern of self-restraint. But consistent boundary setting is not easily learned. Under a subhead, "Establishing Boundaries with Yourself," Cloud and Townsend suggest these steps:

- Address your real needs.
- Allow yourself to fail; learn from consequences.
- Listen to feedback from others.
- Surround yourself with loving and supportive people.[7]

If a situation directly affects you or other members of your family, you need to define your boundaries. If only your adult child is affected, you need to let him go with the consequences of his choice.

How do you know if you need better boundaries? Here's one test: If you find that you and your spouse have more than the usual conflict after your divorced child visits or telephones, the tension may be a by-product of insufficient boundaries. Parents with healthy boundaries protect themselves and their marriage from the power plays of a thoughtless adult offspring.

Unfortunately, many parents find it hard to say to their adult children, "I love you and I do not want to ... (whatever is being manipulated)." Dora and Kurt recalled how, after nearly a year of intergenerational living, they had to almost push Brad and his preschool son out of their home. Brad did not take ownership of his parenting responsibilities as long as his parents would "parent" for him. New boundaries were needed.

Another dad, Craig, a successful fifty-something attorney, was upset when he learned that his divorced son had dropped out of law school (for which Craig was paying the tuition). Craig "owned" his feelings and penned a truthful yet respectful message: "I'm disappointed to learn that you're not returning to school. For now, I'm sure you'll learn a lot at your job cutting diseased trees for the forestry department. Mom and I will use the money designated for your tuition to fly to see you in Montana. Would the opening of trout season be a good time to come?"

Having definite boundaries means you do what you feel good about even if it's not pleasant, such as sitting through a day in court with your adult child. And it means refusing what you do not feel good about, perhaps refusing to accept sleep-over partners or vile language used around your younger children.

God is the perfect role model for boundaries. He is a God of order and meaningful relationships. As Christians, we're born into his family and long to reflect his image. With the guidance of the Holy Spirit we can be self-controlled and freedom-giving parents.

LIFESTYLE ISSUES

Life issues of sexual behavior, substance abuse, and stewardship of money are serious life issues. Parents want their children to be mature in these areas. When daughters or sons show immaturity, parents are impatient. But if you want someone to change, the best way is to plant seeds that will grow. Don't stick an idea into your child's head in full bloom and expect it to take root. The graft will wilt and wither for lack of "feeding." Instead, your job as a parent is to "grow" ideas that you can endorse.

Parents are too easily disappointed when "bad spots" show up in their adult children's lives. All people are a mix of God's creation and the blemishes of sin. You may have had control for a short while as your child was growing up, but even then, wise parents let their offspring make their own decisions and live with them. When adult children stray off the path of healthy living, they learn best by dealing with the consequences. Parents are guides in life, not shields. "You continue to love your sons and daughters, to pray, and to offer counsel and help," writes author David Veerman in *Parenting Passages*. "But you are not responsible for what they make of life. If they mess up, it's not your fault."[8]

Whatever the error of his ways—substance abuse, sexual sin, or financial irresponsibility—your adult child has only stumbled; he's not stymied forever. Says author Shirley Cook: "God brings [our adult children] into deep waters not to drown them, but to cleanse them."[9] As he struggles, he doesn't need you on his back, but backing him up. When you wish you could change your child's lifestyle, but know you can't, write out your desires. Use your thoughts as a prayerful petition. Or talk to God about your daughter's life. He will listen to you even if she won't. Meanwhile, your divorced child will be taking a closer look at your life, marriage, and values. You'll be tested to have your *own* emotions under control even when your divorced child does not.

We're called to love our grown children as whole people, not just the parts we prefer. This is a reflection of God's perfect love for all of us. "Get rid of all bitterness, rage and anger, brawling and slander, along with every form of malice. Be kind and compassionate to one another, forgiving each other, just as in Christ God forgave you" (Eph. 4:31–32). For Christians, the playing field of life is level at the Cross.

Part 2

REBUILDING FAMILY BONDS

7

ADAPTING TO NEW FAMILY CIRCLES

Apparently, God thought that creating family was worth the risk. The first family on record eventually became the tenacious nation of Israel. Throughout the Old Testament we learn about Israel's heritage by following its clans and family lines. In the New Testament, the significance of families is reinforced as Jesus declares that Believers are forever one in the family of faith.

Divorce ends marriage; it does not end family. God's love is conveyed in family images: father and son; mother and child. "As a mother comforts her child, so will I comfort you," says Isaiah 66:13. As we love our families, we learn how much God loves us.

DIVORCE IN AMERICA

The percentage of North Americans getting married is at an all-time low. North America has more single parents than any other industrialized nation. Nationwide, 22.9 percent of homes are headed by a single parent. (Japan, France, the United Kingdom, and Canada range from 5.9 to 14.8 percent.)[1] The Census Bureau estimates that more than six out of every ten children born in the United States in the mid-nineties will live in a single-parent home before they reach their eighteenth birthday.[2]

Meanwhile, the number of divorces increased almost 200 percent between 1962 and 1992.[3] Beginning with the "me" generation of the 1960s and fueled by the advent of no-fault divorce legislation in 1970, the divorce curve rose sharply. In a given year in the United States, there are about twice as many marriages as divorces. Some conclude that means 50 percent of marriages in the United States end in divorce. (However, this is "oranges and apples" mentality, according to researcher George Barna, who points out that this data cites two entirely different groups of people. Some people may divorce several times, while some people never get divorced. The extra divorces shouldn't count against lifelong marriages. Barna says that only about one-quarter of all adults who marry eventually become divorced.)

In the past few years the divorce rate has leveled out and even inched down slightly.[4] However, statistics aside, if you have had a divorce in your family, that's one divorce too many for you.

COPING WITH CHANGE

Like all systems, the family is always undergoing change: it is never static. Birth, death, and the stages between; marriage and divorce; household moves and job changes . . . all this is the stuff of family life. We might even say that the "work" of the family is continual adjustment to change.[5]

Genealogies in the twenty-first century may look more like a rambling rose than a tall tree. Families are hybrids with new varieties in every generation. After divorce and remarriage the family tree is no longer straight and narrow, but complex and interwoven. Love is necessary for continued vine growth, and even more so for the grafted-on branches. When parents refuse to make concessions to changing family configurations, love is stripped from the vines. After a divorce in your family, you will want to consider your own interaction in the new family circles.

Roy Fairchild, author of *Christians in Families* writes, "The family is a sensitive organism similar to the human body . . . it is actually changing day by day. . . . Any serious change that affects *any* one member of our family, affects each of *us* because we are bound together."[6] Divorce within your family is a serious change. New configurations are needed. As parents, you have choices to make about which connections to former in-law children, their parents, and extended family you'll keep. In some cases you may want to hang on. In other cases "amputation" is necessary. You'll have some mourning to do as you let go.

The increase in divorce in the latter years of the twentieth century has caused everyone from parents to political leaders to look for ways to counsel bonding, rather than breaking, of vows. Counselors and clergy wrestle with the ripple effect on the second generation—the adult children of divorce (ACODs).

What cultural changes concern you about family life in the United States? How might you help deflect undesirable trends?

Author Dr. Edward Beal says that, contrary to current thinking, divorce is not the crucial factor in how well ACODs turn out. "It is the kind of family you come from, the way its members relate to each other, the patterns of behavior you grow up with and, unwittingly, imitate or rebel against, that are more likely to influence who you become."[7] It's not the divorce in their background that makes it difficult for children of divorce to achieve intimacy as adults, says Beal, "It is their family style that makes the difference."[8]

Describe what you think your family might be like twenty-five years from now. Does your mental picture help you process change?

"The kind of family you come from. . . ." That's you, the parents of the middle generation. The measuring rod is out. The patterns of behavior you now model for your divorced children, and for their children, have far-reaching influence.

RELATING TO THE EXES

If your adult child's former spouse has remarried, you have a solemn challenge to accept the new family configuration for the sake of your grandchildren. Your thoughtless words can affect the children's attitudes toward their two sets of parents.

Walter and Evelyn Schaller's former daughter-in-law, Liz, wanted their help to buy a home. "If you love your grandkids, you'll do this for us," Liz told Walter, who was in the real estate business. The Schallers made the down payment, with Liz agreeing to meet the monthly mortgage. Later, the Schallers saw that Liz was unable or unwilling to be a responsible provider. Walter foreclosed the mortgage and served an eviction notice. The Schallers ended up with their son and grandchildren living with them for three years.

But new family relationships can also thrive. Patty's remarried former daughter-in-law still invites Patty to her home for the grandchildren's birthday parties. Patty shared with me how well her former daughter-in-law's new husband relates with the kids. Unexpectedly, she blurted: "It makes me so angry!" *Why anger?* I thought. Patty read my mind.

"Well, my Claude was never able to get down and tumble around as the children's stepfather does. The kids love him!" she explained. Underneath her honest anger, Patty was glad her grandchildren had a happy two-parent home to grow up in, but she was also fighting the loss of her dream for her own son.

Nowadays, as adult children divorce and remarry, it takes more commitment than ever for families to "keep the covenant" with one another. Your former in-laws may make moral choices radically different from your own, such as two men or two women "parenting" your grandchildren. Or, your divorced son or daughter may live continents apart from an ex-spouse and still "share" children back and forth.

Margaret Freeman, a pastor's wife, confided that she was stretched beyond her imagination when her divorced daughter married for the third time. Each son-in-law had come into the Freeman's family circle with children of his own. Going further than most couples, Margaret and her husband make an effort to keep in contact with all former grandchildren who are not of their family line. The Freemans' picture-portrait in their church directory proudly shows *all* their grandchildren— including steps, present and past.

Mary Ellen in Nashville says that losing her son-in-law was like experiencing his death because she was so close to him. Her daughter, Lynette, didn't want to be home when her "ex" came for his belongings, so Mary Ellen agreed to come over to house-sit. Mary Ellen recalls the day: "When Graham saw me, he grabbed me and hugged me, and said, 'I wouldn't have done this to you for the world—but I am.' The next day he moved away. I've not seen him since. Time does heal, but during holidays I find myself wondering how he's doing.

Lillian, a mother we met in a previous chapter, also talks about her relationship with her former son-in-law. She told her daughter Casey: "I consider Daniel as my son. I love him, just as I love you." Lillian says Daniel has no family, so she's been his mother—a role she intends to continue.

If your door is always open to an former in-law, it's best to have permission from your divorced son or daughter. Seeing your child's "ex" secretly will cause irreparable harm to your parent-adult child relationship. At the least, listen to their feelings. Before you hold firm, be able to give your son or daughter clear reasons for why you want to continue having contact with their ex-spouse.

> *If you're fond of your former son- or daughter-in-law, will you let go of that relationship? Why? Why not?*

Krista and Larry grew to love their daughter-in-law, Mieko, years before her marriage to their son, Paul. She had been a young exchange student from Japan and lived in their home. Later, she returned to live and work in the United States. As the years went on, Paul fell in love with her. He learned Mieko's language, visited her family in Japan, and they were married in a storybook wedding. The marriage lasted about four years.

Krista hurt not only for her son, but for the daughter-in-law who had become so much a part of their family. "For awhile Mieko would come over here and just hold tight to me and cry. But she wouldn't talk about the split. I felt so left out. I couldn't keep guessing about where things stood," says Krista. With Paul's permission, the two women met for lunch. Although the divorce had proceeded despite Krista's fervent prayers, now she began to accept the reality: "I saw the incompatibility, the unrealistic aura in which they married. I was sad, but I finally understood."

When Mieko was packing up to return to Japan, Krista wrote her, asking her to visit the family one last time. But the pain was too great for Mieko. Through Paul, Mieko asked that his family not contact her anymore. "I was so sad . . . I cried most of the day," Krista recalls. "I wanted to beg Mieko to see us before she left the country. I tried to use Paul as a 'go-between,' but he set me straight. 'Mom, you're just making it more painful,' he told me. 'It's all I can do to get up and keep going each day.'

"We've all lost something," Krista says sadly. "There's a lot of pain for everyone."

DIVORCE AMONG ETHNIC FAMILIES

For several years my husband and I lived next door to a large, gregarious family from Turkey. Their sprawling backyard was filled with relatives and friends nearly every weekend. Grandmothers rocked babies. Wives prepared mounds of ethnic foods, from shish-ke-babs to sesame seed salads. The men seemed mostly to sit, smoke, and sip.

Surely with all their friends and acquaintances, I could find a Mediterranean family to interview about how they handled divorce in the family. Not so, Silvia said. "Our young people get married—not too young. They have babies, and they stay married."

I'm sure there are exceptions to Silvia's observations. First-generation Americans may in fact be more apt to divorce than relatives in their homelands. Yet, the number of divorces seems to be significantly fewer for families who honor strong ethnic values.

In two large Chinese congregations, I found few parents to interview about divorce. Those I located had attempted to blend two cultures and the Chinese parents felt that marrying outside of the culture was a major factor in the failed marriage.

The divorced Chinese I did talk to found it difficult to be socially accepted by their single Chinese friends. After their divorce, they had to go to another church—a Caucasian congregation—to find a divorce recovery program. This, of course, increased the likelihood of another mixed marriage, which concerned Chinese parents.

Accepting divorce in the family was difficult for the Chans. Peter and his wife, Ruth, both in their mid-fifties, have a large family but never expected to face divorce. Few of those in their close-knit Chinese community in the San Francisco Bay area asked why their daughter Laurie and her children had come home. It seemed more polite to say nothing.

"If Laurie weren't a mother, maybe we could let her go it alone," says Ruth, as we share a lunch in Chinatown. "But we'll do all we can to help them survive," Ruth goes on to tell me how she and her husband helped Laurie get A.F.D.C. (Aid to Families with Dependent Children) food stamps, and some free medical care.

"We know that answers to our prayers for Laurie can come through other people, not just us, her parents," Ruth adds. "I rejoice in any progress! In the book *Something More*, Catherine Marshall said that her job was to ford the streams with her children, then dry them off and send them on their way. That's what we're trying to do for Laurie."

GRAFTING NEW BRANCHES

Women, more often than men, are the kin keepers attempting to hold families together amicably, even after a family divorce. Mothers and daughters of all nationalities telephone more often, write more letters, and send more cards and gifts.

Mexican-born Leonor is tenacious in her determination to pass on positive family values despite her own marital problems, the demise of her daughter's marriage, and the responsibilities of caring for two little granddaughters.

On Christmas Eve, Leonor felt happy. Even though Jorge had lost his job just before the holidays, this Navidad would be special. The table was covered with an embroidered cloth and more poinsettias than Leonor could afford. Tamales would steam gently all night. Turkey with chilies were ready for the oven, and bowls of sweet flan cooled on the back porch. Tomorrow, after a big feast, everyone would cheer as neighborhood children whacked at a candy-filled piñata. It would be a wonderful day to remember.

Tonight Leonor had taken the Christ Child out of the crèche set up under the tree. She hid the baby Jesus in a place hard to find. Tomorrow morning when Angelita and her husband Raphael came, their two little girls would delight in searching for the baby Jesus so they could put him back in the manger. What excitement!

About eleven o'clock, just as Leonor checked the back door lock, she heard a knock at the front. Who could it be at

this hour on Christmas eve? Jorge had gone to bed long before
Leonor finished in the kitchen. Their fifteen-year-old son had
dropped off to sleep with his headphones on. Then she heard
a baby cry.

"Angelita, is that you?"

"Yes, Mama. Please, I have to see you."

Leonor's heart filled with fright. What could be wrong? Her
hands trembled as she unbolted the door. From the dark night
her daughter and two little granddaughters stumbled into her
home.

"I didn't want to worry you, especially since daddy's lost
his job. It's Raphael's drinking. He promises to quit, but he
doesn't. I just can't cope anymore."

Angelita and the girls spent the night. Everyone tried to be
happy as the family went to Mass and opened gifts on Christmas morning. But Leonor worried about the future.

A trailer parked in their side yard became a temporary
home for Angelita, but she felt confined and controlled by her
family's values. While she longed for emotional support,
Angelita said she needed to live independently. Although this
was hard for her parents to understand, Leonor and Jorge
moved "their girls" to an apartment close by.

In confession and counsel, Leonor tearfully asked her
priest, "Why does this divorce happen to our family? . . . Maybe
I do wrong as a mother?"

"God helped you to be a good parent," Father Joseph told
her. "You are not responsible for the poor choices your daughter's family makes."

Leonor had done the best she could in raising Angelita.
When father and daughter had differences, Leonor soothed
Angelita's feelings: "Your father is a good man. He's strict
because he loves you and your brother." Maybe Leonor herself had been overprotective when Angelita was a teenager, but
only because she worried about her safety.

"We want you to finish getting your teaching credentials,"
Leonor told Angelita after the separation. "Although your

grandfather in Mexico did not know how to read and write, all of his children are now professional people. You can be too. We'll help with books and some baby-sitting. If you are rich you can lose money, but education you keep forever."

It's been a hard three years since that Christmas Eve crisis. Angelita brings the girls to Leonor by 6:30 A.M. three days a week. Their grandmother gives them breakfast before the oldest catches the school bus. Then she takes the youngest to preschool. When Angelita has evening classes, Leonor prepares dinner for everyone, and the girls stay with their grandparents.

Imbued with traditional values in a world that sometimes treats those values lightly, this wife-mother-grandmother daily lives out her convictions. Says Leonor: "You don't have anything, if you don't have family."

Read Genesis 12:2–3. Give thanks to God that your family is included in the Lord's blessing to Abraham. What family traditions do you encourage?

What attitudes hamper the dad in the following role-play from accepting changes in his family? What kind of relationship do think this father and daughter will have three years from this scene?

Cast: Dad, conservative, middle-aged father; Sara Jo, divorced daughter in her mid-twenties, dating a Cuban

Scene: A summer evening in South Carolina. Dad's garden.

Dad: It feels good having you working with me in the garden again, Sara Jo. I've sure missed you the past two years you've lived in Miami.

Sara Jo: I've missed you too, Dad. Although you keep busy at the medical lab, I know you've been lonely since Mom died. It's hard being alone. I hope that can help you understand how much I appreciate my friendship with Manuel.

Because of him I see that my life can go on. I really want you to meet Manuel soon.

Dad: Do we have to talk about your Cuban friend? I just keep hoping you'll understand that your worlds are too different. Your brother, aunts, uncles, and cousins are all here. I wish you'd come back home to live.

Sara Jo: When I went to Miami after my divorce, I couldn't see much beyond the cotton fields. Now I know that life holds many equally good choices. I'm falling in love with Manuel, Dad.

Dad: Manuel may want to go back to Cuba to live. When you have children—they would be half Cuban! Your family ties are right here in Carolina, Sara Jo. We raised you in the church—the same one your grandmother belonged to.

Sara Jo: I'm glad you mentioned church, Dad. When I first met Manuel, I told you he's a Believer. I've been going to services with him, and you'd be pleased to see Manuel's strong faith.

Dad: But does he understand *our* ways of worship?

Sara Jo: One thing the church taught me was to love everyone in the family of faith. Until recently, I really didn't know the full meaning of that. I've grown a lot spiritually, Dad. I hope you can see the good side of things happening in my life.

Dad: I could put in a good word for a med-tech job for you here in Lancaster.

Sara Jo: Sorry, Dad. I don't know what the future holds, but I've learned that goodness is a matter of the heart—not a certain way of doing things. I hope you'll come to see that too.

By what measuring rod do you judge your divorced child's friends? Read Colossians 3:12–14 and pray for a gracious heart.

THE FAMILY MOBILE

As one parent with two divorced daughters said, "Divorce is surely not God's best, but I'm learning to adapt to *what is*." Rev. Campbell, father of Shana, says that we "cannot hold our children legalistically in a bad marriage just to please us as parents. We can learn one generation from another how to forgive and go on in love."

As I observe our seven-month-old grandson, Kyle, lying in his crib, he gives me a child's definition of the family in flux. Kyle intently studies the dangling black-and-white family figures on a mobile hanging above him. I point out the miniature mother swinging to and fro, with her bushy black hair and a stark white apron. "And, look, Kyle, here's the daddy," I say, touching the largest figure in striped black-and-white coveralls. Children of several sizes are delicately hooked on the fragile trapezoid. Family members, along with their black dog and white cat, twirl in sustained suspension.

Could Kyle's chubby little fingers grasp one of those enticing figures dancing above his head? I watch him swat the air without success. He reaches higher and higher. The lower figures spin with dizzying speed.

Finally, with the tenacity of a determined fisherman, he locks on to one figure. Kyle looks startled, like most of us with an unexpected prize. The mobile, with the detached member no longer in place, hangs sagging, limp and lifeless. The bounce is gone because the balance is missing.

How like our own families, I muse. Although Kyle sees only amusement, a deeper truth is that when one member is displaced, the rest of the family is affected. But the allegory ends there. For the mobile, the solution is a mechanical one, to hinge the piece back the same way it was before the disruption. For a real family, that solution won't work. Families are growing and evolving organisms. They can never fit back exactly the same way once they've changed positions. It's up to other members of the family to adapt.

Change is never easy, especially if we're not the ones initiating it. The definition of "family" today is changing so rapidly we seem to bob in space as our "family mobile" goes up and down, round and round. Many children now have six or eight grandparents, instead of four. Multiple marriages add step-this and in-law-that. Are the former in-laws whom our grandchildren still call "mom" or "dad" in balance on our family trapezoid—or spinning in space?

If history is any indicator, the family will continue to change. Parents of divorced adults must adapt to those changes or forever be out of kilter. Family stability depends on committed emotional attachments across the generations.

A definition of family by author Edith Schaeffer will anchor the family through winds of change. She says that a balanced family has "unity and diversity. Form and freedom. Togetherness and individuality.... A Christian family is a mobile blown by the gentle breeze of the Holy Spirit."[9] Caring families are strong stabilizers in a fractured society. They know how to redraw the family circle with arms of love.

8

ENCOURAGING THE HEALING PROCESS

After a divorce in a family, raw emotions often flood in and fracture parents' link to their adult children. Healing is needed. Family ties, the most intense of all life relationships, are worth nurturing. Our family connections may profile our best self and, without work, our worst.

Crucial to this "work" is learning about our own past. When we shut ourselves off from our heritage we pinch our emotions in much the same way as we would pinch our fingers in a closing door. In the Gospels, the apostle Paul likens life to a footrace. If we're weighted down by the past, we lag behind and lose the prize.

"The past is powerful, confronting us more than we care to admit. The past fashions the way we think, respond, and act. The past cannot be altered or forgotten—only examined, explained, understood, and reckoned with,"[1] say authors Jerry and Mary White in their book *When Your Kids Aren't Kids Any-*

more. Understanding the source of our attitudes gives us a healthy perspective.

Making peace with the past separates clear "now-centered" thinking from murky "then-centered" patterns. Negative responses may be part of a pattern you learned as a child or adolescent. Psychologists Henry Cloud and John Townsend call these "sins of the family" and suggest confession, repentance, and change.[2] Making peace with our family of origin (birth or adoptive) is primary in becoming a whole person—at any age.

Claire Helix talked about her distressful relationship with her parents. She feels that past hurts contribute to poor connections with her own two daughters, both divorced. Claire's mother died before Claire realized that making amends with leftover childhood experiences would help. Hoping to "square things" with half of her parentage, Claire wrote a long reconciling letter to her father. "But it was too late for that too," Claire said wistfully. "His memory was gone."

When I began writing this book I had no idea if any of my mother's brothers and sisters were still living. When I was very small my mother married again and moved from Appalachia. Poverty, the austere years of Word War II, and general apathy left our family ties dangling. Now, studying the importance of family heritage, I was motivated to look back. It took only a few spadefuls of genealogy to locate four aunts I hadn't seen for more than half a century. In phone calls and exchanges of old photographs they rounded out my somewhat distorted image of my late mother. I appreciate her more deeply by seeing her through the eyes of her siblings. Now I can pass on this nearly lost heritage to my own adult children and grandchildren.

CONNECTING BACK TO YOUR GENEALOGY

Connecting back to your roots is a pilgrimage in search of yourself. You may find your dominant family patterns are hostile and conflicting, or perhaps condescending and conforming. Either way, you will see how relationship barriers are passed down from one generation to the next. For example, if you hold your son or daughter at a distance emotionally, it may be because that's the way you've been unwittingly taught to think about parenting. If the women in your family were traditionally homemakers and now your divorced daughter wants a Ph.D., only by releasing the patterns of the past can you fully support her ambitions.

Family faces are like magic mirrors. By looking at people who belong to us we can see the past and present and muster hope for the future. Unfortunately, few of us are brave enough to bring our distorted memories into clear focus.

Jim, a forty-year-old divorced Englishman, talked to me about having felt abandoned by his parents, who had sent him to boarding schools. During a holiday at home, he discovered that his father had left Jim's alcoholic mother. At ten, Jim missed his father terribly and blamed his mother for breaking up their family. Now, years later, Jim has difficulty relating to women, including his adult daughter. Leftover forsaken feelings from Jim's chaotic childhood have erupted and clouded the present. He exposes his fragile feelings: "Buried deep within me there's still a fear of commitment. I'm afraid I might be deserted again."

Soon after Jim's divorce, a counselor directed him to write out his angry thoughts toward his deceased parents and lay those letters at their headstones. As Jim wrote, he was first able to forgive his father. Later, he began to see his mother as a beautiful woman as well as one addicted to alcohol.

Although I was not close to my maternal family and located my paternal ancestry only after I had children of my own, I always carried a "fantasy family" in my mind. While I belittled and buried the past, emotionally I longed to confirm that I belonged to someone, somewhere. Like thousands of other hurting people, for many years I used secrecy as a tool for "forgetting" the past, until, like Jim, I discovered that problems can only be faced when they're out in the open.

Using genograms—mapping information about your family as far back as possible—is a tangible and graphic way to trace family patterns that may shed light on either your or your children's present behavior. (Although compiling genograms has been around as long as family therapy, new computer programs make it much easier. An inexpensive one, "Family Ties,"[3] creates ancestral and descendant trees.)

Genograms structure information in a nonthreatening manner. Assembling this fascinating puzzle, your very own portrait, takes on a certain mystique and excitement. It's the widest possible view of your family's history, like seeing photos of Earth taken from outer space. A long-range look nearly always changes rigid opinions and increases understanding.

Our past is also the history of God working in our lives. It is His-story, as well as our story. Family shortcomings are absorbed by God's overwhelming love. Dealing with disappointments deepens our dependence on God. We can see that he carried us through the deep waters of the past and that, if we seek his counsel, he will also direct our future.

Consider the following role-play regarding a discussion between Viola and her daughter, Colleen, about Viola's past.

Cast:	Colleen, newly divorced daughter; Viola, her married-again mother; Lester, Colleen's stepfather
Scene 1:	Dinnertime, in the kitchen

Colleen: My therapist says it would be helpful to learn more about my past—like, well, what caused the breakup of your first marriage, Mom, when I was just a baby?

Viola: *(In a sarcastic tone)* There you go again talking about "my therapist"—like she's part of your family or something. Why does she need to know anything about us? You waste your hard-earned money trying to talk away problems. My life hasn't been a bed of roses. I took my lumps, now you can too!

Colleen: I'm sure you must have reasons for believing that therapy can't help. But I know I'm stronger now, so I'm going to keep going. My counselor is a wise Christian woman, whom I admire. It would be helpful if we could all talk about our past ... How about you, Les? You look a little worried.

Lester: Well, yeah. I guess I was just thinking one ought to let sleeping dogs lie. I don't see much sense in going backward.

Colleen: You're both so stubborn it makes me sick! I don't know why I even try to talk to you. It's a waste of time. You're so narrow minded—and afraid too. That's it, you're just scared to be honest. Forget dessert, I'm out of here!

Scene 2:   Dinnertime, in the kitchen a week later

Colleen: Thanks for calling and inviting me to dinner tonight. I just want you to know that I'm sorry for spouting off and leaving in a huff last week. I don't want our differences to destroy our relationship. Forgive me for hurting your feelings.

Viola: You know that a mother always loves her daughter, even when she gets big notions in her head.

Lester: *(Whispering loudly to Vi)* Now, Vi, don't start picking on that girl again. You'll cause her to slam the door behind her, just like last week.

Colleen: Oh, don't worry. I decided before I came tonight that I'd be patient. I'm not perfect, but I'll try to understand your fears too. What if we agree to begin again?

Viola: I'd like it if your therapist kept her nose out of my business—that's what I'd like.

Colleen: It seems you don't like her, even though you've never met her. I'd like to invite you both to come with me to a counseling session and see for yourself what it's all about.

**Lester and
Viola:**   *(Nearly at the same time)* Us come?

Viola: *(Hesitantly)* Well, I don't think so.

Colleen: Okay, I'll ask you again later, though. For now, I want you to understand that learning about my childhood would mean a lot to me. I hope you'll consider talking about it someday. That would please me very much. . . . Let's dish up supper.

   Why do you think Viola was unwilling to talk about her past with her daughter? List the various negative and positive responses. Did the family members understand one another's perspective? How do you think that learning more about your family history and passing your heritage on to your grown children would make a difference in all of your lives?

DIG OUT RESENTMENTS AND FAMILY TRIANGLES

The word *resentment* comes from two Latin words meaning "to feel again." The description fits. Grudging parents allow bitterness to flood their emotions long after they've been hurt. A grudge can be used as a way to punish our adult children by driving an emotional wedge between the generations.

Just as every resentment against your son or daughter is an offense against God, who loved them enough to die for them, your forgiveness is a bridge that, with God's love, can reach across any breach. David Augsburger says it succinctly: "Caring and honest-ing; that's the Jesus way of working through differences."[4]

Milton, a father who had always been generous to his son, resented that Jason never mentioned the unpaid loan Milton had given him to start a new business after his divorce. The business failed. "I could see that the money was lost," Milton tells me, "but I still wished my nonchalant son would say he was sorry."

Instead, Milton stewed silently. Maybe he could have cleared the air with Jason in a brief interchange, but he always lost his nerve. Finally, realizing that his suffering was his own, Milton consciously chose to "forget" the loss and to stop hoping for the return of the money. Humbly, he asked God to forgive his deep resentment over his son's negligence. When Milton turned his mind from pain and toward life he saw Jason with new eyes.

When one person in the family feels animosity toward another, and instead of going directly to that person for resolution goes to a third person, hoping to "feed" negative feelings, unhealthy triangles form. A collusion of two persons, shutting out a third, complicates communication.

Author Tim Stafford sees triangles as a "deflection of intimacy—[because] a third person keeps us from engaging in the face-to-face conversation we so badly need."[5] Although family members may occasionally crisscross to seek counsel and perspective, extended triangling is a roadblock to vital relationships.

Sometimes the third person in the triangle is seen as the victim (usually the passive one in a divorce). Other times, the third person is seen as the villain (usually the initiator of the divorce). Whether formed to help or to oppose, ongoing triangles usually propagate incorrect information and stymie the resources of the "villain" or the "victim."

---

*If you have formed unhealthy triangles
instead of resolving issues,
what can you do to "de-triangle"?*

The most common triangle is a parent and adult child colluding against a former spouse. Multigenerational triangles also form when a divorced adult brings her children "home" and you begin to share in their care. Siblings may triangle with a former brother- or sister-in-law, thwarting family solidarity. These distorted relationships are a barrier to healing throughout the family. If you are aware of triangles in your family, you may need prayer and counseling to untangle the unhealthy alliances.

WORK AT FORGIVING

Sometimes we're bound to our grown children by unhealthy guilt. Guilt is a turmoil that can be altered only by forgiveness. "Healing occurs when our memories no longer recreate the feelings of hurt from the facts of the past," says psychologist Archibald Hart.[6]

The mortar of forgiveness is acceptance, beginning with accepting your own feelings and attitudes. Ask yourself: "Can I forgive myself? Can I forgive my son or daughter, their ex-spouse, in-laws—anyone connected to my pain? Can I forgive God for allowing this to happen?"

You may find it difficult to forgive your adult child's serious offenses—lying, deceiving, stealing. And if they're not repentant, it's even more difficult to forgive. Barbra Minar, my author-friend whose son was estranged from his family for several years, says she learned to forgive when she realized that forgiveness was for *her* healing.

As parents, we're tempted to excuse our grown children. In *Forgive and Forget*, Lewis Smedes cautions: "Excusing is just the opposite of forgiving. We excuse people when we understand they were not to blame. . . . We forgive people for things we blame them for."[7] Author Gordon MacDonald adds, "To forgive is to withhold judgment, forswear vengeance, renounce bitterness, break the silence of estrangement; to actually wish the best for the person who has hurt us."[8] That doesn't mean your relationship with your divorced son or daughter will be immediately transformed, but it does make a new beginning possible.

The authors of *Forgiving our Parents*, *Forgiving Ourselves* outline these five steps of forgiveness:

- Recognize the injury.
- Identify the emotions involved.
- Express your hurt and anger.
- Set boundaries to protect yourself.
- Consider the possibility of reconciliation.[9]

We can experience forgiveness even without our adult child's cooperation. Our part is to offer our own reconciliation: To initiate forgiveness, a parent might say, "I'm disturbed that I called you names I didn't really mean. You are important to me. Please forgive me." But a response cannot be predetermined. "We *will* to forgive. We promise not to remember. The rest is up to God."[10]

Forgiveness is not natural, nor is it easy. Forgiveness is a decision not to be bitter any more. Time heals, but only after forgiveness has been given. Forgiveness sets us free from the past and allows us to focus on the present.

Forgiveness is not an event, it's a process. Cleaning out emotional attics takes time, and we're bound to disturb some dust in the process. Begin the cleaning with, "I want to be closer . . . and I'd like to find ways to make that possible."

If the situation surrounding your adult child's divorce generated resentments, it's never too late to forgive. Divorce is not an unforgivable sin. God's Word—from Genesis to Revelation—affirms God's grace for every human weakness. God forgives; we are to do likewise. Praying for the courage to forgive is possibly the most meaningful prayer we can pray.

CONSIDER THERAPY

Parents of divorced adults usually do not seek therapy even though they may feel (rightly or wrongly) some responsibility for the breakup. "It's okay for Johnny (or Sally) to go for help, but it's just something we have to live through," I often hear parents rationalize.

*After your child's divorce,
whom do you need to forgive?
Is there a relationship that needs closure?*

Last year, as part of a "New Hope" Christian twelve-step program offered by my Santa Ynez Valley church, I became part of the miraculous process of restoration, as people with arrows lodged deep in their hearts allowed caring and praying friends to help pull out the throbbing barbs. Because of this small-group experience, I am more sensitive to the pain behind many stoic postures.

If you feel despondent after your son or daughter's divorce, consider therapy for *you*. In counseling you can think out things, discover solutions, and avoid pitfalls. And in a support group, you'll meet others who have been through similar situations. These people won't see you as a failure—either as a person, or as a parent. They'll care about you and they'll be no farther than a phone call away. Allow Christian friends to shore you up when you plan to tell your daughter, "I cannot let you live in our home with your boyfriend, but I can loan you my car on Saturday to check out available apartments."

Sophia and Herbert thought they knew the answers to almost anything—until they were faced with grief of their son's divorce. When their son announced he was divorcing his wife to live a gay lifestyle, they knew they needed help. In therapy, this couple learned to adapt and take life as it comes, not as they wish it were.

A number of singles told me their parents disdain their struggles. If your adult child's problems—such as lawlessness, drugs, abuse, homosexuality, or suicidal thoughts—are foreign to your experience, it's too much to just expect them to "snap out" of it. Instead, help them get the professional counsel they need.

Alma and Fred, whose son recently married for the third time, had to learn that it takes some children longer to grow up than others. Their son went through two divorces before he joined Alcoholics Anonymous. In the process of healing, he has learned to control the compulsive behavior that had contributed to his broken marriages. Now Alma believes there's real hope for him and their new Christian daughter-in-law.

As your child releases negative feelings she can better face the real world. Until Laurie, a single mom, was in a recovery group, she shared little with her parents, the Chans, even though they lived in the same house. Laurie's participation in a "Fresh Start" group helped her break down emotional walls. She talked about how prayer had helped release her bitterness and anger.

If your divorced child has a severe dysfunction, your grandchildren are likely to ask you questions: "Why is my mom in therapy? Why can't I go visit Dad?" Be careful that your answer is nonjudgmental and easy to understand. You might say, "Right now your mom (or dad) needs to get well and this is the best way. We can all help by being patient." Don't increase suspicion by closing off further conversation; instead say, "Let's talk about this again in a few weeks."

Suffering in the family is never an individual matter. Divorced children often have some unfinished business with their parents. If you are asked to be part of their therapy process, willingly cooperate. You will surely profit from several sessions of family therapy. It's an opportunity for you to develop new relational skills.

Remember, the key to therapy is finding solutions, not "fixing people." In family encounters you'll learn things you never imagined bothered your adult child. It's not so important that the therapist understands your viewpoint (perhaps creating a triangle), but that family members understand themselves and one another.

Family counseling is far more effective than a self-run family forum because of the safe, controlled environment moderated by a non-family member. The counselor is everyone's trusted advocate. When family members feel their opinions are heard, they're willing to risk new patterns of relating.

In *Multigenerational Family Therapy*, author David Freeman lists the major long-term goals of family therapy:

- Improve the ability to deal with and accept differences
- Improve problem-solving abilities
- Develop a balance between individual autonomy and family solidarity
- Work through unfinished business[11]

Where can you go for help? Unfortunately, Christians may limit themselves to a few sessions with their pastor and ignore the long-term work needed to fully restore relationships. A church usually has a list of professionally trained therapists, as does your medical doctor. The book *How to Find the Help You Need* by Archibald Hart and Timothy Hogan is a good resource.

Choose a certified counselor with the same care you would a surgeon, lawyer, or other professional.

Consider the advantages of therapy—for yourself, your adult child, and for the whole family. What would you look for in choosing a counselor and/or a support group?

In a chapter titled "When It's Too Hard to Do It Alone," author Shauna Smith fills two pages with criteria for choosing a therapist who specializes in family therapy. She suggests looking for someone who: encourages a relaxed atmosphere, treats you with respect, has fees within your ability to pay (covered by your insurance), suggests options without telling you what to do, is accessible by phone, communicates warmth and caring, can be a role model.[12] You'll also want someone who respects your Christian worldview.

As you grow emotionally, changing attitudes and ways of interacting, share that information with your adult child. Until you clearly state your new position, everything you do will be twisted by "old tapes." Your son dents the car and you say, "I can't understand what happened!" He hears, "Dad thinks I messed up again." Try to unearth feelings underneath the facts; say, "You must feel terrible!"

Encourage your adult child in her own growth. As you see new patterns emerge, tell her how much that pleases you. With the guidance of the Holy Spirit, parents can be Christ's ambassadors for reconciliation that will affect future generations.

RECONNECTING BRINGS HEALING

Probably our strongest life attachment is to our children. They come from our very being, and that is a connection that remains despite all trauma. In times of dissension, here's one suggested formula: "Act directly, act dispassionately, act without delay."[13] Reconnecting keeps problems from growing larger. Swift amends assures sweeter memories.

In every tragedy there's a kernel of healing. Arthur Maslow, coauthor of *Family Connections*, describes what is needed for healing family relationships: an atmosphere of openness, guidance, and acceptance of failure; parents who model adjustment to circumstances; and growth that allows family members to move on with their lives.[14]

But attempts to reconnect don't always lead to immediate reconciliations. In extreme cases, such as chemical dependency, criminal charges, or serious psychosis, you may need to erect temporary, protective boundaries. I talked to parents whose divorced son or daughter had just "vanished," without any good-byes. Others had adult children who, although living relatively near, seemed unwilling to be part of the family. If you're one of these parents, prayer may be the only connection to your child for now.

Through prayer, God connects us to the "bigger picture" of life. Author Henry Cloud says it well: "People who are attached, bonded to God and to others . . . have an increased ability to handle stress and their life accomplishments have meaning."[15] In connecting with God, you can learn to minimize the regrets of the past and make healthy changes in your own life. In time, you may be privileged to reconnect with your wayward daughter or son.

In closing, let me leave you with this insight: Family interaction and connectedness is akin to a good game of Frisbee. How so? Well, when the light-weight plastic disk was introduced in Great Britain, one competitive onlooker became more and more puzzled. To the English gentleman the sport seemed like an unending round of "throw and catch," no one stopping to tally points. Who's winning?" the bystander finally shouted! "No one," was the reply. "It's the back and forth that counts."

9

MANAGING ANGER AND BUILDING TRUST

Families will always have conflict. The apostle Paul, writing to the church at Ephesus, says: "In your anger do not sin." No, that's not a contradiction. Paul also defines sin as "giving the devil a foothold." And he warns us: "Do not let the sun go down while you are still angry" (Eph. 4:26–27). Do you feel comfortable with the idea that anger is acceptable? That it can be openly owned? That it is a normal, natural human emotion?

Divorced children have a lot to be angry about as they fight custody suits, deal with attorneys, and are denied visitation with their children—all the while hoping to heal from wounds inflicted by being severed from someone they once loved. When they come to visit their parents they hope for an oasis of calm in their stormy lives.

What is the atmosphere in your home? Can your adult children and their children drop in anytime and find you are just the same as you've always been? Even coming for a short visit they may feel apprehensive, wondering what your mood will be. If they find you critical and accusatory, they'll respond with defensiveness—and anger.

Read Hebrews 12:15.
What "bitter roots" have caused trouble
between you and your divorced child?

Most parents want to be *less* angry, to feel closer and more at ease with their children. Yet we're human, and especially vulnerable with our grown children. We easily find fault and are frustrated when values collide. Parents have an uncanny way of cutting off an adult child's attempt to express his feelings, attitudes, hopes, and dreams. Before he's able to get it all out, we jump in with a "perfectly obvious" solution or answer.

ANGER IS A CHOICE

It is easy to become angry when grown children do foolish things. Maybe we even accuse them of exasperating us on purpose. The truth is, we *choose* to be angry. If expressed in wrathful words that cannot be taken back again, anger is a shortsighted choice. Defensive anger seldom changes the situation or the people involved.

If you often find yourself angry, stop and consider the source of your anger. What specific feelings precipitate conflict? Do some soul-searching before you confront your adult child. "Trying to resolve a problem before we have identified it . . . is like attempting the high jump wearing work boots. To identify what is blocking us . . . is not a luxury; it is an absolute necessity."[1]

Dr. Neil Warren, former dean of the Graduate School of Psychology at Fuller Seminary in Pasadena, California, counsels that the first step in handling anger is getting your self-concept in shape. "The better you feel about yourself, the more effectively you will process your anger,"[2] Warren writes in *Make*

Anger Your Ally. When you feel good about yourself you have
the energy to think through your problems and, because you
feel positive, fewer encounters will frustrate, threaten, or hurt
you. Problems arise when you get "stuck" in unresolved anger.
Coauthors of *A Handbook for Parents*, Robert and Alice
Fryling, say that parents "often hide behind anger because we
want to believe we are powerful, self-sufficient, important and
perfect; when, in fact, none of us is like that all of the time."[3]

If anger can be useful but also destructive, how do you tell
the difference? The Frylings give four characteristics: Good
anger is slow, restrained, short-lived, and forgiving.

ANGER CAN BE MASTERED

With desire and determination, anger toward your grown
children can be mastered. Anger is a useful servant uncovering
the need for changes in a parent-adult child relationship. It can
heighten the emotional commitment to make things better
between you. Well thought-out anger-expressing strategies lead
to growth.

Anger comes from frustrated emotional demands. The key
to controlling anger toward your adult child is understanding
the buried feelings that cause those inner irritations. No question is more basic than "*Why* am I angry?" Learn to say in a con-
versational tone what you feel and what you want of your son
or daughter.

Conflict is neither bad nor good; it's simply a part of life
in honest relationships. David Augsburger's coined term, "care-
fronting," assumes that conflict is "natural, normal, neutral, and
sometimes even delightful." This Mennonite pastor says that
"how we view, approach and work through our differences
does—to a large extent—determine our whole life pattern."[4]

Focus anger on your adult child's behavior, not on his personhood. Augsburger recommends that caring must come first,
before any confrontation. Caring means that you are "truly *for*
another, genuinely concerned *about* another, authentically
related *to* another.... The crucial element [of care-fronting] is—

does it foster growth? Does it invite maturity? Does it set another more free to be?"[5] In a caring encounter a parent considers an adult child's views before unloading parental partiality.

How can you handle your angry feelings when your adult child is moving headstrong toward trouble such as an explosive relationship, job failure, or negligent parenting?

A closed mind will not build a solid relationship with your adult children. While parents need not sacrifice conviction or truth, we may get hung up on unhealthy prejudices and pride. Through care-fronting we can work at changing our mind-set within moral boundaries. Good care-fronting clarifies the important issues.

If your adult child insults you and you're tempted to respond in an outburst of anger, stay committed to a care-fronting framework. During the heat of battle listen to your inner self as well as to the barrage against you. Direct your mind to form forgiving thoughts toward your bullheaded child. Before you retaliate, find something in his or her list to *agree* with. Nothing diffuses anger like agreement, even if it's only agreeing with one small part of an angry accusation. The apostle James gives parents good advice in his first letter: "Lead with your ears, follow with your tongue, and let anger straggle along in the rear."[6]

Communicate your own feelings with "I" messages: "I feel anxious when . . . I'm hurt because . . . I'm frustrated by . . ." Accentuate the positive along with your specific complaint. For example, Henrietta learned to tell her son: "I know you're a good father, and I get angry when you bring the kids over here and let them run wild!"

Anger can provide the power to get at the source of problems. In fact, says Dr. Warren, "Anger can help you discover the deepest and most satisfying levels of meaning both in relationship to others and to yourself."[7] Your adult child will sometimes feel angry toward you, sometimes affectionate. Both sides are acceptable to God and, hopefully, to you.

If resolution seems impossible, avoid prolonging the fray. Don't let your adult child become a long-standing enemy. When you sense things are getting out of hand, try saying, "Son, I don't see this discussion benefiting either of us right now. If you have some new information, I'll be glad to talk at another time, but right now I'd like to change the subject."

> *Write down some alternative ways to discuss controversial issues with your adult child and still preserve your relationship.*

To keep conflict at bay, some parents deny it exists ("Our family is as happy as most"), brush it off ("Things only get out of hand now and then"), or wallow in guilt ("I guess I'm just a poor parent"). The truth is, parents need to be skilled negotiators. In resolving conflict you are trying to make peace with your children. "Your task is to break down the wall between you . . . not to add bricks to the existing wall, or to do battle. The best way to remove a wall is to simply take down your side of the barrier with grace and humility."[8]

Manage conflict or it will manage you. A graceful way to produce a wise agreement, be efficient, and not damage a relationship is to negotiate, say two Harvard University professors who wrote *Getting to Yes*.[9] I've expanded their basic points into "Seven C's":

- Clarify the issues: separate the people from the problem.
- Convey love: focus on interests, not positions.
- Consider alternatives: invent options for mutual gain.
- Choose a win/win plan: evaluate possible solutions.
- Confirm the follow-up: make sure everyone understands what to do.

- Confidentiality: do not replay problems to others.
- Counseling: agree to get professional help if needed.

A soft negotiator gives in too easily; a hard negotiator keeps an iron will. The method outlined above proposes being hard on the merits, soft on the people. It enables parents to be fair while protecting themselves from being taken advantage of.

LEARN TO NEGOTIATE

As we've already discussed, families have ongoing patterns. In an authoritarian family, only *one person* wins. In a democratic family, only *one side* wins. In most families, everyone mistakenly thinks he knows what everyone else thinks about a controversial issue. Hope for real understanding lies in learning to negotiate. Consensus is a win/win method created by clear mutual agreement.[10]

Explore new methods of resolution. For a parent, even sitting in a circle rather than at the head of the table, is helpful. Agree on the ultimate goal, such as better understanding or preserving relationships, as well as a workable solution for a specific situation.

Before negotiating, first, talk about the process of negotiation—such as everyone taking turns listening without criticism. Second, predetermine the time limit for negotiating to discourage someone from stalking out later. And third, agree on the nature of the core issue. Write out and refine the wording until everyone agrees on what the *real* problem is. (If several major conflicts exist, deal with only one per session.)

As parents, you can set the tone. Bring dignity to the arena of dissension by inviting your adult child to be a whole person. Say, "Give me both your 'cold pricklies' [honest anger] and your 'warm fuzzies' [affirming love]. Let both of your faces show." Tell him sincerely, "Both sides are important. Both are acceptable. Both are precious. Both can be loved."[11] Tell him you'd like to help make things better. If your discussions are unusually volatile despite these precautions, a third party is probably needed to mediate successfully.

Brainstorming is a swift way to come up with several options for action. Consider all ideas because, in a family forum, we can only learn what others are thinking when everyone feels free to express their ideas. During brainstorming you may find yourself admitting to prior nearsightedness.

Only when time is up, or when you seem to run out of ideas, is it permissible to begin evaluating what you have come up with. Shirley Campbell, a professional arbitrator, calls this "CPR" time—resuscitation of "Content, Process, and Relationships." If your adult child consistently roadblocks all ideas, you'll need to deal with that problem before you can move ahead. (His unwillingness to negotiate may stem from perceived assaults to his self-esteem.)

The chosen solution is the one that's least discriminatory, one that gives everyone at least some benefit. It may not be a perfect plan, but it should seem worth trying. All solutions are renegotiable, of course, but the chosen plan should be followed until everyone agrees it should be changed.

Everyone involved in the negotiating needs to know how to follow through. Ask each person to state his understanding of the solution. Try to define and diffuse foreseeable minor problems. If it seems that you need penalties for infractions, determine what these should be by consensus.

"Happy are the peacemakers," Jesus said. Maybe he was thinking about parents who have learned to withstand conflict and not get emotionally burned. Writes David Augsburger: "When [they are] vulnerable . . . people come to life as real, living, breathing, hurting, feeling, laughing, singing, growing beings. Repentant vulnerability is the most consistently beautiful and meaningful experience in human relationships."[12] Peacemaking is a virtue worth cultivating with divorced adult children.

In the following role-play the parents need to consider each other's position as well as negotiate with their single son.

A couple in your group might volunteer to videotape this before your next group meeting.

Cast: Jesse and Mattie Morris, husband and wife
Scene: Living room, early June in Louisiana

Jesse: *(Holding a letter from Seth, who now lives in Ohio; Jesse is excited)* Hey, Mattie, this sounds great! Seth says that since he's been wanting to relocate in Louisiana he'd love to house-sit for us in September and October. He'd water the yard and gather the mail. And he could look for a job too, and get settled. Looks like we can get the motor home rolling!

Mattie: Hold on, Jesse! I suppose it would be great for *him*, but maybe not for us.

Jesse: I hear a real concern in your voice. Something must worry you about Seth staying here.

Mattie: Well, we know he smokes. And he may bring that German shepherd of his. What about that? I just bought a new white sofa. And how do we know he's coming alone? He might be living with Cissy—that girlfriend he talks about so much.

Jesse: *(Frowning)* Hmmm ... I hadn't thought about those things. I hate to just tell Seth no. We'd have to give him a reason.

Mattie: What if he doesn't find a job that pays enough? Once he's made himself at home here, he might like it all too well. You know, Seth isn't the same person he was at eighteen. Really, he's more like a stranger to us, at least in lifestyle.

Jesse: *(Looking at Mattie with care and concern)* How could we feel good about this and be helpful to Seth too?

Mattie: I'm open to talking about it with Seth. I think we need to be up-front and say there are several things to negotiate and agree to before we can enjoy being gone. Could we invite Seth here for a few days over the Fourth of July weekend to talk about all this? You've got air miles saved, so we could send him a plane ticket. Maybe he'd be more sure about relocating if he came to visit first.

Jesse: You've brought up some good points, Mattie. *(Pats Mattie's hand)* Let's call Seth tomorrow and invite him. I see that more understanding would help us all feel better.

How did Mattie and Jesse handle their own feelings and react to each other's feelings? Were they supportive of each other? How might they negotiate with Seth about house-sitting issues? Do you think, come November, this family will be better friends?

BUILDING TRUST

Parents so easily lock into a framework of "what was, will always be." It's crucial to all adults' emotional well-being to have their own ideas and beliefs. Parents sometimes forget that it takes enormous emotional energy for adult children to become self-confident people.

Your divorced daughter may be afraid of losing your love if she doesn't please you. Although you may try to shore her up with free housing, money, and a job, these support beams sag in significance when she sees your disapproving frown or senses your unspoken shame.

"Spun out" divorced children may also be tempted to become too dependent on their parents, depleting their self-worth. The authors of *Boomerang Kids* list things parents can do to help their grown children "individuate"—become their own person:

- Empathize with them.
- See their [divorce] as a temporary setback, not a permanent failure.
- Accept their emotional responses.
- Encourage them to develop confidence and competence.
- Respect their autonomy.[13]

You are—or can be—a significant prototype to your grown son or daughter. Parents are privileged to be "forever models," while other archetypes in your adult child's life come and go. Parents will be replaced only when they don't deserve the honor.

Look around your home. Do the photos on your wall and in your wallet idealize the past or affirm the present? When your adult child walks into your living room, seeing an up-to-date photo of him (and his family) is more of an honor than a photo of his high school graduation.

When your daughter comes to your home to visit, do you focus on seeing the grandchildren (assuming she is a parent)? Your daughter needs to know that you care about spending time with her too. And when you talk about things one-on-one, take advantage of the total communication not possible by phone or letter. Let your facial expressions, intonation, and touch convey your love and concern.

Let your adult child know that you trust him. In your trust he will feel your love, acceptance, and respect. David Augsburger says, "distrust tightens the chest with anxiety, burns in the throat like smog, tears the eyes with its acidity, and poisons the whole person."[14] On the other hand, trust—breathed in an atmosphere of love—nourishes us like oxygen. In patient trust, parents need to listen and weigh their words before releasing them.

Mike and Gail, in Little Rock, Arkansas, had to overcome a lot of anger and resentment after Leanne's divorce. "We were the only couple we knew who had a divorced child!" Gail exclaims. "All I could see was a fatherless family," adds Mike. "We had to grab hold of the fact that the world had not come to an end for Leanne—or for us."

At first, Mike felt disgusted at his daughter's mistakes and choices. "It was a prideful thing to see her in need," he says, "but I knew 'saving her' would only damage her self-esteem in the long run. I learned to keep my silence and depend on the Lord to open her eyes to new pathways." Both Mike and Gail talk about how it was hard to learn to trust their daughter's decision even as she began showing more maturity.

Near the beginning of the apostle Paul's second letter to the Corinthians he used the Greek word for "comfort" ten times. He writes about "standing alongside" to encourage another during severe testing. When we comfort our adult child, bolstering him with our trust, we give him a priceless gift.

"The two arms of genuine relationship," says Augsburger, are "confrontation with truth and affirmation with love."[15] Parents who learn to master their anger, manage conflicts, and establish lines of trust, provide their divorced child with the bedrock to rebuild self-worth.

10

POLISHING THE FRIENDSHIP BETWEEN PARENT AND ADULT CHILD

Divorce in your family took you by storm. In time, the wild winds will blow away. When they do, will you be better? Will you be stronger because you stood against the turbulence? Will you be able to be friends with your divorced son or daughter, truly love this adult child, and have a contagious hope that affects your entire family? Yes, you will—with a little work.

You start by being a friend.

BE A FRIEND

Harold, a fair-haired American, clumsily twiddled chopsticks between his fingers at various angles all evening. Halfway through the many courses of his Chinese dinner, he gently suspended the slender sticks parallel on his plate. I sensed that

Harold had a pronouncement to make. "I want my grown kids to be my friends!" he said emphatically. "Like learning to get these chopsticks in sync, I want to move in rhythm with my daughters' feelings—especially with Abbie, since her divorce."

I hope this is your challenge too. Parenting has seasons, and having adult children is the final evolution of your role as a mother or father. And because you are intimately related to your divorced son or daughter, you can be a one-of-a-kind friend.

Parent-adult child friendship can hasten post-divorce adjustment. Research shows that "the absence of stresses among supporting family members and approval of the divorcing person's decision" are very important for recovery.[1] Times of struggle cause us to lean on one another. There's truth in the adage: Broken eggs make a better omelet.

The bedrock for friendship with your divorced child is how graciously you can allow him to be his own person, yet "be there" for his support. If you think back, you'll remember that from their earliest responses your children told you they wanted to be recognized in their own right. "Me do," said your toddler. "Don't need a hand," said your school-age son. But when the hurts came they wanted you close by. Divorced adults still want a parent's comfort. Take this opportunity to get reacquainted at a deeper level.

A PARENT-FRIEND VALUES RELATIONSHIP

Your adult children carry around an inner judgment about what sort of parents we've been to them, and still are. In fact, many singles tell me they feel as if a parent is looking over their shoulder from thousands of miles away. Parents have awesome power!

We can expect too much of our grown children. We imagine them getting honors in school, finding a good job, and having a "happy-ever-after" marriage. But life is a mixture of the wished-for and the unwanted; the hoped-for and the unfulfilled. Just as parents wonder whether they should have helped a teenager more when he brought home a C-minus on a biology report, they will probably wonder if they should have done more to help his "grade" in marriage.

Both you and your divorced child need to see that the failure of a marriage and being a failure are not one and the same. This trying time is not necessarily a reflection of weak inner resources.

Often, being a parent-friend to divorced singles means "going with the flow" of their ever-changing life. Although you may express true feelings of surprise, disappointment, or regret, ultimately you will want to encourage them in their journey. In the following role-play, how does Alex's dad's respond as Alex reveals a new direction in his life?

Cast: Alex, twenty-six-year-old divorced single son; Alex's father
Scene: A warm summer evening. Alex and his dad have just finished shooting some baskets in the driveway hoop they put up years ago.

Alex: Hey Dad, you're still in pretty good shape. Keep it up!

Dad: I feel more like working out when you come by to shoot a few. I really look forward to our scrimmages.

Alex: Dad, I need to tell you that I won't be able to come regularly any more. I enlisted in the army a few days ago. I'll get my report orders by the end of the month.

Dad: Now that's a shocker! I'm surprised you didn't discuss it with your mother and me. We thought you were doing really well selling auto parts. It looked like you had a district managership nearly in hand. What happened, Son?

Alex: To tell the truth, I've been restless since my divorce last year. I know I don't want to be a salesman all of my life. I like working with things "hands on." The army needs mechanics, and I need some direction. The military is good security.

Dad: I'm curious. What did the recruiters say about the ring in your ear . . . and those tattoos on your chest? And what about the pair of greyhounds you care so much about?

What will become of them? There's a lot to think about here, Son.

Alex: *(Smiling)* Yeah, the earring will have to go, but the tattoos passed my medical inspection okay.

Dad: Alex, although your marriage failed, Mom and I have prayed that you could use the things you learned and begin again. Your good job seems more secure to me than an unknown stint in the military. But even though I'm disappointed we didn't talk about this earlier, I know the choice is really up to you.

Alex: Thanks, Dad. I hate to leave in lots of ways. But I have to have a clean slate right now.

Dad: Alex, no matter where we go, our "slates" go with us. Only God's grace truly gives us a new start. That's what your mother and I have been praying for you right along. Maybe this is just a different answer than we expected to our prayers.

Alex: Dad, even when we're on way different wavelengths, you've always been a friend. I know you and Mom pray. Although I haven't always followed suit, I appreciate that you care. Hey, they have chaplains in the army. Maybe I can catch their worship services on the base. I'll write you about it.

Dad: Well, about those dogs. If Mom agrees, we'll keep them for you. It's the least we can do for a friend.

How can you be supportive to your single son or daughter when their life takes unexpected turns?

Your divorced child may have personality patterns that jar you. Look for reasons behind his criticism, sadness in his anger, and anxiety in his distancing behavior. Unresolved relationship problems with our adult children do not just fade away; they only dig their tentacles deeper until love—God's love—sets us free. During an impasse with your adult child you may feel as if you're just biding time. Instead, use those weeks and months to get in touch with your own feelings of shock, anger, hurt, and disappointment. As you pray, ask God to help you be part of the answer instead of part of the problem.

If your adult child is stumbling along many months after a divorce, are you tempted to think she deserves to falter? If so, you have some things to settle just between the two of you. "If she'd only listen to my advice!" you wail. But your adult child cannot—will not—absorb your advice wholesale. She can only "discover" and use wisdom a bit at a time, when she's ready and willing. You need to be the one to take the initiative.

Make a date with your adult child; tell him you want to share some things that have been weighing on your mind. Praise the progress he's made in his life as a single. Tell him you want things to go well for him—and for you. Then express the ways you wish your relationship were closer. Be prepared to modify your expectations; you may want the impossible. Your attitude, is of prime importance. It is one of the few things you can control. Hold yourself accountable.

> *List your hopes for the relationship between you and your son or daughter (I wish that we . . .); list hopes for yourself (As a parent I want to . . .). Decide which issues you want to deal with and a plan of attack for each one (I worry too much when Marla calls only about once a month. I'm going to make it clear that I need her to . . .). Date your wish list and keep it as a benchmark to measure future progress.*

"Easy love" is fluid and soon forgotten, even in family circles. Beware if your wish for reconciliation is so strong that you'll do almost anything. You may get sucked into a controlling situation. The difference between out-of-control reactions and deliberate responses is offering acceptable choices.

Bernice Walker, an African-American woman wise in faith, knows that growing a family takes time. "We can experience forgiveness, grace, and new beginnings, yet the friendship needs time to develop," she said. Bernice believes that friendship develops most naturally by being vulnerable with one another, growing together.

Whatever your family's "testing points," the Bible is a good place to find renewed direction. On a "down day," find a reassuring verse. Write it out and tuck it in your pocket. "Watering" the family tree with Scripture is sure to bring nourishment to the branches.

Read Ephesians 4:3. What are the qualities that "keep the unity of the Spirit through the bond of peace"?

Does a parent ever have the right to say to an adult child, "I won't be supportive of you any longer. I won't root for you, trust you, anymore"? "Only when they have come to the end of their parenting," says author-pastor David Augsburger. Only when parents choose to say, "Stop the family; I want to get off."[2]

When you heal your differences with an adult child, your spouse and other family members are more apt to mend their own emotional fences too. Whether at the end of a day or at the end of your life, you'll be grateful you helped reforge the severed links in your family circle.

A PARENT-FRIEND HELPS SORT THROUGH SITUATIONS

"I hate how James promises the kids something and then doesn't follow through. I just won't be home when he comes for them next weekend!" your daughter rants in a diatribe against her ex-husband. How can you keep yourself detached from your adult child's problems so that she can keep ownership? Stay neutral and help your daughter sort through the situation.

Think of yourself more as a teacher than a parent. Teachers ask questions that bring new perspectives. Ask probing questions that will help your daughter sift and sort her ideas. Ultimately, she must own the choices left in the hopper. Trusting her to act wisely gives her the courage to forgive her "ex," to take on new responsibilities, and to deal with her children's problems.

Likewise, when your divorced son talks about his "ex," his children's attitudes, or his present friendships, be attentive but nonjudgmental. Feed back his concerns and tell him you're praying for him. Let him come through the fog with his own sense of direction.

When you know your adult child is genuinely concerned about a pending decision, take it seriously also. Express your interest: "Dad and I have been thinking about that business venture you've been exploring and we have some ideas. Could we plan to talk tomorrow night after dinner?"

Read Ephesians 4:15–16. What is it that holds the body—and families—together? What will help you and your divorced son or daughter to hold together, grow together?

When you talk, ask questions that require content answers, like, "What's the most challenging thing about your new job?" Listen to the answers; don't interrupt. Occasionally repeat a key word to encourage more dialogue. If there's no response, try to find out what blocks the circuits between you. Ask if your questions are helpful. Are you asking too many questions? Not enough?

As our divorced sons and daughters struggle with feelings of abandonment, emptiness, and failure, they want us to see them as people, not merely as products of their circumstances. Friendship blossoms when you say, "I'd like to run alongside you in the unpleasant skirmishes of life."

A PARENT-FRIEND BELIEVES THE BEST

Many years ago you learned to recognize the various cries of your infant. Mad, hurting, hungry? You knew. Now, decades later, you decipher your adult child's mood through his tone of voice and body language, regardless of his words. Some adult children may want your counsel, but pretend they don't. Some may pretend to heed your advice, yet have no intention of taking it.

"You never see me for who I really am!" your adult child accuses. And you retort: "You never listen to what I say!" Neither expression is fertile soil for love and respect. Love is an active expression, and communication is the love line.

As you look for ways to polish your friendship, be careful about "self-talk"—the ways you think about your divorced child. If your inner assessment is negative, you may act out what you believe to be true. If you know that negativism is a pressure point for you, take an inventory. Each evening, recall the unnecessary negative tracks your mind has taken. Then jot down all the positive things you can think of about your daughter or son and give thanks!

Read 3 John 4. In what is parents' joy? The next time your divorced child seems to be down on himself, tell him you really believe in his abilities.

Savor quality time that deepens your adult-to-adult friendship. "Let's go for a walk, or spend a weekend in the mountains," you might suggest. As you discuss life, you can pledge 100-percent support, and receive the same, even while still disagreeing.

Nothing enriches a friendship like truthful, insightful praise. Make praise a constant refrain. Remember to say things like, "I'm proud ... Congratulations ... Way to go! ... I love you." A good relationship depends on loving affirmation. Without it, old garments will be put on again, like rusty armor. Adult children will lighten up when their load of failure is balanced with a parent's sincere praise.

A PARENT-FRIEND VALUES INPUT

Throughout this book you've been encouraged to create close bonds with your adult child. But a bond doesn't mean emotional bondage—for them or for you. Be vulnerable; occasionally ask for feedback. After a weekend together, ask what they liked and didn't like about your time together. Then listen nondefensively.

When you're shopping for a car, making an investment, planning a vacation, buying a pet or a computer, ask your adult child for his advice. Showing that you value their input may move your relationship from merely politeness to becoming a pal.

To be good friends, your adult children need to know you as a real person, not as a "leftover" parent. While you want to be proud of your grown children, you want them to be proud of you too. If you've made a significant lifestyle change—perhaps you've become a Christian or recommitted your life to a deeper faith—explain your redirection.

The table game "Life Stories"[3] provides a comfortable and fun way for parents and adult children to talk about their life journeys. An adventuresome family might try some role-playing such as described in this book. Or just let your adult child sit at your place for dessert some evening and, in good humor, pretend to be you. You, of course, play his part. Have fun parroting his pet phrases; you'll hear some of your own from him. If you videotape the scene, play it back and laugh (and cry!) while sipping coffee after dinner.

An ideal motto for parenting is writer William Glasser's definition of friendship: "The ability to fulfill one's needs in a way that does not deprive others of the ability to fulfill their needs."[4] To be a friend involves, ultimately, a willingness to take on our son or daughter's joy, sadness, or desperation. True friendship forgives the past, enjoys the present, and focuses on hope for the future.

A PARENT-FRIEND ACCEPTS THEIR CHILD'S OTHER FRIENDSHIPS

Two-thirds of divorced women and three-fourths of divorced men marry within three years after their divorce. When your son or daughter is considering remarriage, don't expect a replacement of the prior spouse. Look for a totally new thing God is doing in his or her life. The desire to handle the give-and-take in a new relationship is often a sign of healing. That's reason to rejoice, not to fear.

Parents have no right to manipulate, or even strongly hint at, their wish for a particular partner. However, it's thoughtful to suggest that your single may bring a guest to family events and holiday celebrations. Don't fret if they bring no guest at all; they're rebuilding their life in their own time.

If you have a legitimate specific concern about someone your adult child is dating, ask questions that help him or her ponder the issue. "Is Don planning on changing jobs soon?" you might ask your daughter about a boyfriend who seems restless about his employment. "Tell us about Madeline's desire to grow spiritually," you might inquire of a son who seems smitten with new love. As you talk, your adult child will likely voice some of his own silent concerns.

Are you more comfortable with your divorced child remaining single, or do you wish he or she would marry again? Why?

When your son or daughter is seriously dating a single parent, occasionally include the friend's children in your family get-togethers. If your adult child marries that friend, you will have "instant" new grandchildren. Many children of divorce feel excluded from remarried families. The sooner you help them feel comfortable, the better.

Sometimes, for various legal or economic reasons, previously married people decide to live together. Christian parents feel more uncomfortable about living-in arrangements than do nonreligious parents. If your children make this choice, honor them apart from their lifestyle decision.

Your concern for your adult child's relationship to Christ is more important than trying to control his social relationships. If he's not a Christian, his morality will likely bend to popular views. If he is a Christian, you may lovingly point out the inconsistency in his standards. Having done that once, let it be.

A PARENT-FRIEND IS FUN-LOVING

Include your single (and his children) in your family-fun times. Ideas are not limited to your pocketbook. Think "outside the lines" and creatively celebrate life. Trips to missions, a retreat weekend, a concert, or jointly sponsoring a third-world child give mutual interest and pleasure to three generations.

The more physical activities you share, the better. Friendly competition works off tension. Try sports like golf, hiking, or tennis. Buy a table tennis set or a new piece of exercise equipment to share. Take an inexpensive day hike to bird-watch, or, if you can afford it, travel to Colorado for a family ski weekend.

In *The Recovery of Family Life*, Eldon and Pauline Trueblood write of bonding through a simple, shared meal. "The table is the center of the home," this husband and wife team says. "There are many beds, but only one board. . . . The breaking of bread is potentially a holy act."[5]

Begin a weekly game night (but don't take it too seriously). Rent a family-night movie; keep the themes light and funny. Play word games—even by mail or Internet. Buy matching T-shirts to wear to a family outing. Write a tongue-in-cheek script for a family celebration. A cartoon bulletin board in your home will keep everyone laughing. Take turns awarding a blue ribbon for the zaniest find.

Use catalogs for family shopping next Christmas. Having gifts taken care of is a big relief to singles. When the order arrives, arrange a "wrap-up" night with a festive dessert. Be creative in your gift giving. (A hint: Give your divorced child a gift of time instead of a monetary gift. "Four hours during January to. . . ." List some options and a blank for their own suggestions. You may find yourself mending, helping cook, giving a perm, or providing some other personalized "gift.")

Be careful about giving books and tapes with a preachy message. And if it's your idea to give a weekend at a Christian conference, offer a brochure along with other alternatives— not a prepaid reservation. When single son Kirk told his parents, "I know I should get back to God," they heard an answer to their prayers. Later, Kirk's parents used their credit card to pay for a weekend conference that Kirk *himself* said he'd like to attend.

As you interact with your adult children you build trust. For example, after playing together you'll feel more comfortable sharing a problem heart-to-heart. Play, laugh, and have fun together. Enjoying good times with your single son or daughter will deepen your friendship.

A PARENT-FRIEND LETS GO

The largest number of respondents to an informal radio poll—44 percent—indicated that parental control was their most disturbing intergenerational problem. James Dobson of Focus on the Family, sponsor of the poll, summarized the feelings of these adults toward their parents: "I still love you. I still need you. I still want you as my friend. But I no longer need you as the authority in my life."[6]

Our adult children's lives are shaped more by failure than by success. When we do not release them, we deprive them of their personhood. Separation, freedom, independence—whatever word you choose to launch your adult child again— implies that a pleasant emotional distance is mutually agreeable. "Letting go" is one of the most difficult things parents must do. A parent is prone to protect. But a top priority of parenting is to prepare your offspring for the day when you will no longer be part of their earthly family.

In describing "letting go," the authors of *Adult Children Who Won't Grow Up* suggest that parents

- encourage adult children to make their own decisions;
- allow them to struggle and grow at their own pace;
- admit that the outcome is not in your hands;
- release outdated images of yourselves and your adult children;
- foster emotional health throughout the family.[7]

We may have to accept that we'll never have the ideal child—or adult child—we envisioned. If need be, allow yourself to grieve over your lost dreams. Realize that they were just that—dreams. Your friendship with your adult child will flourish if you focus on *their* dreams, not on your own illusions. Popular author (and grandfather) Chuck Swindoll is adamant about living his life in reality: "I would much prefer to live my life on the sharp, cutting edge of reality than dreaming on the soft, phony mattress of fantasy."[8]

> *In what ways have you "let go" of your
> divorced child? In what ways do you still hang on,
> limiting his freedom as an adult?*

Psychologist Arthur Maslow believes that a "balance of interdependencies" marks healthily bonded families who have learned to let go. These families are "dependent on one another as parts of the same system, yet they're also independent as individuals. . . . There's a physical and emotional distance between the parents and their grown children that allows the members of both generations to grow and develop."[9]

In his book *Powerful Personalities,* author Tim Kimmel says God blesses parents who let their children be independent.

If parents fail in this, Kimmel believes that God allows the consequences of meddling and control to haunt us throughout the rest of our lives—even to our last days.[10]

When we let go of our adult children, we set them free to be themselves. We continue to care about them, but not *for* them. We emotionally support them, but don't control. When our grown children sense our belief in them, they are more likely to return the adult-to-adult friendship we ourselves offer.

Harold, the active grandfather whose story opened this chapter, did find fun things he and his daughter and grandsons could do together. The spring that Abbie brought her young children home to live, they planted a garden and watched the seeds sprout, then blossom. To Harold, the garden became a symbol for the furrowed family growing toward new maturity.

Like Harold's garden, becoming a family is a journey, not a destination. Although parenting has a beginning point, it has no ending point short of death or debilitation. It is the ultimate life experiment! You don't graduate beyond parenting. Other friends can be found, but parents as friends are irreplaceable.

11

LINKING THE FAMILY THROUGH GRANDPARENTING

My husband, Russell, and I have just spent the past two weeks enjoying being active grandparents. Although the five families (with eleven grandchildren) that we visited have intact marriages, there's a generic nature to grandparenting. We, along with grandparents everywhere, realize that looking into the face of a grandchild is like looking into the future. Grandparenting is more than cookies and milk and a bedtime story; it's our legacy.

Because it had been six months since our last visit, three-year-old granddaughter Kelli pondered about who we were. Although we had sent pictures and talked by phone, our appearing at her third birthday party was, in her words, "a little scary." She gave us a pensive once-over. Then, about an hour into the festivities, as I was serving her cake and juice, Kelli's face lit up and her eyes twinkled. "I know you!" she said. "You're *part* of my gam-ma."

Right on, Kelli! I am *part* of her eight grandparents. That can be a little confusing for preschoolers, especially if they don't see their grandparents often. Kids don't get divorced, but a break anywhere in the family structure divides a child's sense of relationships. It's likely that some of your grandchildren have multiple grandparents too. If so, you are only a "part" of their "whole."

PROFILE OF A GRANDPARENT

As a grandparent, you have a lot going for you: experience, wisdom gleaned from both success and failure, and a long-sighted view of time. If you were a grandparent by your mid-forties, you may well be a grandparent for half of your life. Grandparents are healthier, more active, and more financially secure than ever before. Today, grandparents have a sterling opportunity to invest in future generations.

Read 2 Timothy 1:5. What effect did this grandmother have on her grandson?

There are more grandparents now than in any time in recorded history. And according to 1990 Census reports, about 3.2 million children were living with their grandparents or other relatives—an increase of 40 percent in just one decade.[1] These statistics, especially to Christian grandparents, signal opportunities for hands-on care and involvement in their grandchildren's lives.

More three-generational studies are needed to identify new roles and responsibilities within the modern extended family. Meanwhile, Christians can look to Scripture for role models. There's Abraham and Sarah, Isaac and Rebekah. The book of Matthew opens with the human genealogy from the beginning of humankind to the coming of Christ. It shows how families are linked throughout history. And ongoing creation, in continued "begats," will link us to the future.

Pediatric psychiatrist Arthur Kornhaber says that the main function of today's grandparents is to rebuild the family pyramid. "As grandparents go, so goes the family," he proclaims. Kornhaber sees a "vital connection" between the first and third generations: the emotional well-being of children requires a direct—not merely a derived—link with their grandparents, he believes.[2]

In the United States, grandparents are usually called by pet names. Children enjoy inventing their own nicknames for grandparents, such as "Mimi" and "G.D." Such terms of endearment show that American grandparenting is not just status—being a matriarch or sage in the family—but a position of unique companionship between senior and child.

Kornhaber describes ideal grandparents who have close bonds with their grandchildren. He says they

- have an emotional priority on their lives;
- value their families highly and are committed to them;
- are usually expressive people, rich in experience, and full of memories to share;
- are by nature altruistic—sensitive to the feelings of others;
- spend a great deal of time involved in the family;
- are relatively immune to social trends;
- steadfastly defend the youngsters;
- relate well to people of all ages and types;
- are generative people—they are active.[3]

It's difficult, though, say Kornhaber and journalist Kenneth Woodward, for modern-day grandparents to feel needed. These coauthors of *Grandparents/Grandchildren: The Vital Connection* say that typical grandparents feel they are just a rescue team to be summoned only in a crisis.

HANDS-ON GRANDPARENTING

Surely, divorce is a crisis time. Christian grandparents will take the initiative to be as helpful as they can in the aftermath of divorce. Scripture warns: "If anyone does not provide for his relatives, and especially for his immediate family, he has denied the faith and is worse than an unbeliever" (1 Tim. 5:8). Helping may require diplomacy, however. Grandparents in divided families can easily get mixed up in exclusive loyalty to one of the parents, usually their own son or daughter. And although grandparents are "natural allies" for grandkids, they can never replace the parent in a child's mind and heart.

Whatever you choose to do as a grandparent, try to balance your desires and limitations with your adult child's legitimate needs. He may expect more than you can give. Agree between you on what is possible. And remember, when you comfort your adult child, helping *him* feel secure, you are indirectly comforting your grandchildren too.

If you sincerely want to be more than a titular grandparent, count the cost, make the choice to be available, and leave the results with God. That's what Nancy, a Pennsylvania grandmother, did when her son's marriage disintegrated after more than a dozen years of marriage, leaving him with four school-age children.

Nancy began our interview on a familiar note: "When your child divorces, it's an experience worse than death," she says. "My first instinct was to move in and help my son raise his four children. Then the Lord reminded me I'd really be taking care of *five* children. I was still Kevin's mother."[4]

Instead, Nancy and her husband, John, have stayed as emotionally close to Kevin's family as possible, even though their son's company transferred him to another state. John plays chess with the grandkids over the phone. And when Nancy writes or calls the older ones, she sometimes reflects feelings she senses in their somber moods. "I know how hurt you must be that your mom and dad are divorced. But it isn't your fault—it wasn't your choice. Your parents love you, even though they no longer think they love one another," Nancy tells them.

Children's drawings in the book *Grandparents/Grandchildren* vividly demonstrate that children who are not close to their grandparents portray them as specters, childlike dolls, puppets, or bizarre figures gleaned from TV comics.[5] Help your grandchildren to get to know you as real people, with varied emotions. Strive to be more to them than a scary ghost figure or a fairy godparent who brings them goodies.

Did you know that the first Sunday after Labor Day is "Grandparents Day"? Don't wait for your adult families to make plans. Take the initiative and plan a fun day. Give the grandkids some undivided attention apart from their single mom or dad. If your grandchildren are age five or older, involve them in the planning; they'll be more excited if you collaborate.

Your grandchild's other grandparents (maybe two or three other sets), also make their own imprint. Don't try to compete with their lifestyles. Just be true to yourself and do what you honestly feel good about doing. When your grandchild tells you about other gifts and big plans, a "That's nice," is sufficient response. Love is a relationship that's earned, not bought.

How did the hands-on "grandmother" described in Ruth 4:16 undoubtedly affect an entire nation?

In a Baptist Press news release, reporter Irene Endicott tells about a grandmother whose gifts to her granddaughter have all been returned, unopened, by the child's mother. This grandmother is saving the gifts for the day when the child turns eighteen. Then, hopefully, that teenager will voluntarily receive years worth of accumulated gifts sent in hope and love.

Another grandmother told me she had put handwritten family memoirs in her bank safe deposit box, willed to a grandchild she's been unable to see since her former daughter-in-law's remarriage.

What about step-grandchildren? If the door is open for a continued relationship with a former step-grandchild, keep the contact—especially if you were close prior to the parents' divorce. As that grandchild grows into adulthood, he or she will appreciate that you hung in there. You do not need to be ex-grandparents!

HEAVY-DUTY GRANDPARENTING

Sixty-year-old Norma has more than a tenuous connection to the three grandchildren she cares for while their mother works. This three-generation family lives a few blocks from one another in the heart of Arkansas' thick-forested Ozark region. Here indigo mountains fade into pale pink as the sun rises over the peaks, announcing a new day. Crystalline lakes, cascading waterfalls, and secluded calcite caves frame the scenic highway near Norma and Ed's middle-class home. The tranquil setting contrasts with the day-by-day struggle to keep going that portrays Norma's commitment to being a primary caregiver for a seven-year-old and two preschool-age grandchildren.

"Sometimes I just sit and cry because I get so tired," reveals this grandmother as we visit one snowy afternoon during the younger grandchildren's rest time. Norma talks about how her commitment has caused her to lose touch with her own friends. Yet she feels strongly about instilling godly values in her grandchildren. Norma praises the Lord that she can provide home care instead of putting the children in a day-care center. "Every day I tell myself that it's the most important thing I can do."

At the same time, Norma admits that she lives with "constant guilt . . . I fear I'm not spending enough time with my aging mother because I have to care for my grandkids. My husband gets little attention. He doesn't complain, so I tend to neglect him. Then, there are days when I'm not even sure that I'm a good grandmother. I'm too exhausted," she says with a sigh.

"I don't get to *really* grandparent, taking the children on special outings and giving them treats for fun. I have to be an authority figure who sometimes disciplines. That puts our relationship in a different category. Although I didn't wish it, I'm now a substitute parent to them."

Ed, Norma's husband, agrees that there have been many changes in their lives. They've tried to adapt. Instead of canceling their vacation plans last summer, for example, they took their single daughter and her three children with them to the beach. At home, Ed goes to Boy Scouts and Little League with his grandsons, and chauffeurs his older granddaughter to dancing lessons. This strains Ed's self-employed schedule, but he's also committed to "second-time-around" parenting.

If you, like Norma and Ed, are heavy-duty grandparents, recruit other family members for relief help when you run out of steam. Broad cooperation stretches the family circle and gives your grandchildren an opportunity to experience varied lifestyles.

Just as you learn other skills, you may want to bone up on new ideas in parenting. Take a child-development class at a local college. Or, with your adult child's permission, enroll your grandchildren in a co-op nursery.

Consider forming a support group for grandparents of children of divorce. Put an invitation in a church bulletin or senior citizens' newsletter. Meet at a neutral place to eliminate the strain of hosting. Limit the number of participants so everyone can share concerns and creative ideas. Participants' privacy and confidentiality should be assured. Your group might sponsor occasional workshops, inviting professionals to speak. Nearly four hundred such support groups have sprung up around the country to ease the emotional toll of caring for grandchildren. These groups can also help you deal with your own marital conflicts your adult child's divorce may have precipitated.

Sometimes heavy-duty grandparenting puts us in a position of going along with, or having to thwart, our adult child's lifestyle choices. Such is the case in the following role-play.

Cast: Mom; Carrie, Mom's divorced daughter with twins
Scene: A Saturday afternoon in July, at Mom's home

Mom: Your father and I enjoy having the children while you shop on Saturdays. It helps us to really get to know them.

Carrie: I'm glad to hear you say that, Mom. I've been meaning to ask you about keeping the twins for two weeks. Next month Steve is going to a convention in Hawaii and he wants me to go along.

Mom: Well, what a surprise! Is this an announcement of a wedding and honeymoon?

Carrie: I don't think we're ready for that yet. But I'm excited about our being in Hawaii together. It's going to be wonderful!

Mom: It sounds like you've already made a decision.

Carrie: It would be easier if I knew that you and dad would take care of the kids. They can do a lot for themselves after a year in kindergarten. They put themselves to bed whenever they want to go. And they eat whenever they get hungry, whatever they want to eat. If they get too rowdy, just set them in front of the tube. They both said they'd like to stay with you.

Mom: Oh . . . they're already counting on it? Well, two weeks is a lot different than two hours on Saturdays. But if Dad is willing, I guess I'll consider it. They can go to breakfast club and other childrens' programs at church.

Carrie: If the children stay, Steve and I don't want them to go to things at your church. People would wonder why you have them, where I am, and . . . you know, be nosy.

Mom: Carrie, we like Steve as a person, but he is neither your husband nor their father. I don't see how his input carries so much weight. You've occasionally let the children go with us to church before.

Carrie: The twins are getting older, Mom. They're impressionable. I don't want them to be influenced by narrow thinking. There's lots of time for them to discover their own inner meaning.

Mom: I'm sorry to hear you say that, Carrie. Your dad and I feel that our faith is the most positive thing in our life. Without Christ's love, we would find it hard to love others.

Carrie: Are you going to keep the children for me or not? I'd like to tell Steve tonight.

Mom: I need to think about this some more. I'm concerned about
                a number of things. I want you to have a nice vacation, but
                I'm not sure that I can go along with your plans. I need to
                pray for some wisdom and talk it over with Dad. I'll give
                you an answer within a week. In the meantime, could you
                come up with some alternatives? Maybe we can work this
                out so that everyone is happy with the arrangements.

What are some issues this grandmother might bring to
God's altar? Which things are beyond her control? Why does
she hesitate to take on care of her grandchildren? Can she be
honest to her own values, helpful to her daughter, and fair to
her grandchildren all at the same time?

LONG-DISTANCE GRANDPARENTING

With jet travel, no grandchild lives more than a day away.
There's probably no more than a few hours between you and
your grandchildren. Some airlines have programs in which you
can accumulate air miles as you make purchases, even when
you buy groceries—soon you'll get a free flight. Most airlines
also have low-priced coupon books for seniors.

Make a little picture storybook using candid snapshots from
your visit to send after you're back home. Write captions rein-
forcing your good memories of being together. For young children, send good-sized pictures mounted on durable foamboard.

If you have a computer, have your photos developed on a
disk. Then send individual pictures via modem, or mail the whole
disk. Grandchildren with computers can enlarge the pictures on
screen, print them, or copy them onto their personal disks.

Kids like to see pictures of their parents when they were
young. You probably have several shoe boxes with old pictures
stashed away. Occasionally send a dated snapshot to grandchildren (especially if it depicts a similar time or event in their
own lives), such as when your son got an award, learned to
drive, or was all dressed up for the senior prom circa 1980!

Visiting in "lumps" is not the same as sharing daily or
weekly times with your grandchildren. With geographic dis-

tance, be more creative in keeping the contact personal and meaningful. As soon as your grandchildren are old enough for give-and-take conversation, make it a point to call and talk only to them sometimes. When a parent says, "Shannon, this call is for you," listen for her squeal of delight!

> *"Children's children are a crown to the aged"*
> *(Proverbs 17:6). Consider the long-lasting*
> *results of grandparenting.*

Between visits, let your grandchildren know they can call you collect if they wish. You might even want to have a portable phone with an 800 number so you can be reached easily anywhere. However, you'll be disappointed if you expect too much. Grandchildren will probably call you when they *need* something, not just to chat.

Keep a clipping file for teens—cartoons, information about their hobby or favorite sport, or a review of a good, popular movie. For younger grandchildren, instead of just sending a book as a gift, read the pages into a tape recorder (ring a bell as you turn the pages) and send the cassette along with the book. You might make an age-appropriate half-hour video (with commentary) of you actively participating in your favorite sport or hobby. (After all, haven't you watched a lot of home videos of their bath and bed routines?)

When you travel, send postcards from the state or country you're visiting. Even before they can read, write "personal" on the front. Enclose personal objects in a letter—a pressed flower, a bird feather, colorful stickers, or baseball cards.

Nancy, from Pennsylvania, writes to her grandchildren: "I remember the day you were born. I'm so glad that God gave you to Poppa and Nana. I'm asking God to help you each day." Viola and one of her high-school-age grandchildren have code names for writing to each other.

List ways that you can bond with grandchildren who are too far away to see often.

Consider creating a monthly or quarterly family newsletter. Ask various grandchildren to send you news and photos about their activities to put in this exclusive edition. With desktop computer technology and good photo reproduction, you can create an interesting layout. For faster, more sophisticated communication, you might link up with older grandchildren via a "family home page" on the Internet.

PLANNING SPECIAL OCCASIONS

Grandparents may be more helpful during the holiday season than at any other time. Everyone is supposed to be happy and merry, but emotions are fragile. Carols and holiday decor may bring poignant memories of better days. Beginning with Thanksgiving dinner, look for ways to bind up the broken family.

Julia, a grandmother who loves to decorate and cook, offers her home as neutral ground on Christmas Day. But she doesn't dictate who will be there. "That's not my prerogative," she wisely notes. Julia sends holiday invitations after her divorced daughter decides whom *she* wants to include. Written invitations minimize misunderstanding. Even then, remember, you're not in control. Giving of yourself without expectations during this unpredictable, emotionally laden time is truly unconditional love.

If you cannot handle the cost of a big holiday dinner, being a martyr will only cause you lingering resentment. Yes, you can have potluck—even for a festive occasion. The important thing is to be together and build new memories of shared family times.

You may wonder whether to take your grandchildren to visit their great-grandparents in a nursing home. While youngsters can bring rare joy to an elderly shut-in, there are considerations. Can your parents cope with the excitement of younger children? Will you need to confine your visit to a small room or can you take a wheelchair into the garden? If you go, plan a visit that has meaning for all.

Millie's grandchildren were frightened by oxygen equipment in the nursing home that looked foreign and foreboding. "First one child started to cry, then the other one got scared," Millie said afterward. "I should have explained about the things that are helpful and useful for people this age."

To a preschooler, even wheelchairs and walkers may look like they belong in a haunted house. When visiting at a nursing home, stay only ten or fifteen minutes and, even then, be sensitive to signals of stress. After the visit, encourage your grandchildren to ask questions, make drawings, and tell others about their experience.

What special family times and celebrations can you plan with your grandchildren? Make a list of things to do together.

Don't make the same mistake that Sylvia, from San Diego, did when she took her grandchildren across the border to Mexico for the day. Because she hadn't taken along documentation of the divorce, proof of custody, and written parental permission to have the children in her charge, she was detained for a couple of hours. From the border patrol office, Sylvia finally located her son by telephone to vouch for her identity.

Other grandparents had difficulty reentering Toronto, Canada, after a trip to Holland with a minor grandchild. They had only passports, not documentation of relationship. The delays at the airport were not only embarrassing to them and disturbing to the youngster, but they missed their connecting flight to Vancouver as well.

GRANDPARENTS' LEGAL RIGHTS

If a parent has custody rights, a grandparent at least should have "customary rights." No matter how you feel about your adult's divorce, you have compassion and concern for your grandchildren. A by-product of fragmented families is that sometimes grandparents must resort to legal procedures in order to see their grandchildren.

In 1983, the United States House of Representatives passed a resolution affirming grandparents' rights to visit with their grandchildren. More and more states are allowing grandparents to petition for visitation rights over parental objections. Visitation legally granted between grandparent and grandchild usually depends on

- age and health of the child;
- health and capacity of the grandparent to provide the necessities while the grandchild is with them;
- whether there is a visiting noncustodial parent, and what visitation schedule he or she exercises;
- geographic distance between the grandparent and grandchild;
- school and extracurricular schedules of the child.

If you have long-term primary care for a grandchild, you may want to become the legal guardian. In August 1994, the *Los Angeles Times* reported that the Ventura County Court had awarded custody of a three-year-old grandchild to the child's paternal grandparents. Court commissioner John Pattie believed the grandparents could provide the child a more stable home than could either the biological mother or father. In Wisconsin, state law has required grandparents to support uncared-for grandchildren.

But court victories may be shallow, and judicial solutions can exact dreadful psychological pain. Teenagers often resent a judge determining who visits whom. Laws cannot legislate friendship with your grandchildren. Whenever possible, Christians need to aim conciliation at rebuilding family bonds in the best interests of the child, without going to court. Even with a legal agreement, reopening negotiations when violations occur exposes children anew to cross-family conflicts.

If a grandparent requests visitation with a grandchild who is already visiting a noncustodial parent, that grandparent may receive a "derivative" visitation agreement coordinated with their son's or daughter's visitation rights. If the child's parent is not able to exercise all or part of visitation time (because of travel, health problems, or work requirements), then the grandparent can legally fill in for this otherwise missed visitation time.

Should grandparents have legal rights? Why? Why not?

When the noncustodial parent in a divorce chooses not to exercise visitation rights, the courts may award reasonable time to the grandparent rather than to the parent. However, if multiple grandparents vie for such visitation, courts have been reluctant to create a "ping-pong" environment for the child by having him traveling back and forth between many grandparents.

Savvy grandparents can have certain "rights" written into their son or daughter's final divorce agreement (or added, if the custody issue is reopened). Of course, both divorcing parents must agree to the clause. Once established, these rights remain in effect even if one of the parents remarries or dies.

If children's needs are regarded by the extended family, multiple homes can be a developmental advantage. Kids' lives can actually be enriched by visitation with the "other" parent and with multiple grandparents. Encourage your grandchildren to share their various visitation experiences with you in narrative-like conversation: "Tell me about...." Reinforce their positive experiences in travel, meeting new friends, and trying new foods.

ETHNIC GRANDPARENTING

If your grandchildren have been reared in a dual-nationality family, they may have some ethnic traditions unfamiliar to you. A child's hair style, food preferences, or other personal choices may trouble you. But if you deny things familiar to them, they may be troubled. Ask yourself how much those things really matter. Model your own views and values in the best way you can without denigrating theirs.

If ethnic differences are evident in your far-reaching family, how can you help preserve the positive elements of your grandchildren's heritage?

Grandparent roles have ethnic differences too. Bill Pannell, an African-American and Dean of the Chapel at Fuller Theological Seminary states, "African-American families are more likely than their Caucasian counterparts to take on parent-like roles with their grandchildren. They act more as authority figures than as companions to these youngsters. And they are more likely to discipline than to joke and play with them."[6] Pannell notes that urbanization has added to the duress of rearing children in ethnic families, but there is also a strong ethnic mystique at work. Many African-American grandmothers feel obligated, despite severe economic struggles, to rear their grandchildren after they have reared their own family.

Whatever your nationality or faith, you may sometimes wonder whether you really are influencing your grandchildren. Writers Andrew Cherlin and Frank Furstenberg pose a caveat. They say that grandparents can transmit values to their grandchildren if, and only if, they are first successful in transmitting their values to their children. By their teens, grandchildren seldom share a common worldview with their grandparents unless that view is also embraced by their parents.[7] If there is a shred of truth to this premise, it heightens the importance of parents' relationship with their adult children. As parents, we never stop being a significant role model of life's values to our children, even as they, themselves, learn to parent.

GRANDPARENTING AND THE CHURCH

Grandparenting for the 1990s and beyond has taken on a new definition. Connection to older, caring adults is crucial for the emotional growth and development of children from fragmented families. A child of divorce needs a sense of "we" to hold his or her world together.

However, grandparents may also be divorced. A midlife single person, working full time, may have scant energy to take on active grandparenting. The church—the "forever family"—seems a natural place to deflect this scenario. The Body of Christ can be a gathering point for healthy intergenerational dialogue. Unfortunately, programs in the church are often age-oriented, just as in other institutions. More creative interaction between the generations is called for to help rebuild family bonds.

GRANDPARENTING: A UNIQUE GIFT

Psychiatrist Arthur Maslow, writing about family connections, believes that the grandparent role is almost a casualty in modern America. "Society," he says, "would gain immeasurably if it could find a way to put grandparenting solidly back in the family system."[8] The fault in Maslow's assessment is that he gives the responsibility to society in general—not to individuals in particular.

Whether you live across town or across the country from your grandchildren, you have a unique gift to give them—you. Your time. Your care. Your love. There's a distinctive gleam in the eye of a grandparent. Every grandchild old enough to walk connects to this affirmation. Without strong links between the generations, the ever-present child within a grandparent will shrivel and die. *Winnie-the-Pooh*, shared at any age, can revive a youthful heart.

12

RELATING TO GRANDCHILDREN OF DIVORCE

After a divorce, children often believe they somehow caused their parents to break up. "If I'd only been good enough, maybe it wouldn't have happened," they erroneously think. For these children, a trust relationship with their grandparents provides a platform to assuage their undeserved guilt.

The idea that you're the one who cared for their parent during his or her growing up years is an important concept for grandchildren of divorce. The sense of ongoing caring reaffirms a grandchild's identity and solidifies his trust in family relationships.

THE EFFECTS OF DIVORCE ON CHILDREN

Each grandchild, depending on personality and inner resources, will react to divorce differently. The effects of divorce also vary with the age of each child. Here are some age-appropriate reactions:

- Preschooler: Fears the loss of home, pets, and other familiar things.
- Elementary school-age: Feels abandoned, insecure, and sad.
- Young adolescent: Has anger toward the parent he perceives as the one who caused the divorce. He may feel ashamed.
- Teen: Behavior may be aggressive or withdrawn, both ways of asserting independence. He may worry about finances and other matters of the divorce settlement.

RELATING TO YOUNG GRANDCHILDREN

Be available to young grandchildren as much as possible during the first few months following a divorce in their family. They're probably getting less adult affection than before the breakup. Give them hugs, back rubs, and kisses as casually as you can, without pity or fuss. The emotional strain on young children is apt to cause bed wetting, poor eating habits (either not eating or overeating), erratic sleep, or blatant masturbation. They need time to grieve their loss.

"Do you hate my mother (my father)?" little children may ask. Before you answer, consider that their real question may be "Whom can I trust?" They're looking for someone who is fair and forgiving. If children speak ill about either of their parents, just say: "We'll pray for your mom (or dad)." Show concern, not condemnation.

Young children are particularly influenced by their grandparents' opinions about other family members and their friends. If you oppose new relationships, your grandchildren will wonder why. They'll believe something is wrong that can't be fixed.

In your home, don't put away all photos of your former in-laws. The quality of relationship between you and your grandchild's "other" parent goes a long way toward helping that child maintain roots. When you ask about both their mom and dad, it shows them that you're comfortable talking about *all* of their family. And when they talk about other family members, stay as neutral as possible, accepting their feelings.

During young children's visits, bargain for them to participate in some things that interest you. You'll wear out more quickly if you entertain them only on their terms.

RELATING TO SCHOOL-AGE GRANDCHILDREN

Adolescents are hardest hit by divorce. The family breakup interrupts their "right" to separate from their parents; they feel cheated and abandoned. They think a lot about whether they're destined to repeat their parents' mistake. "Divorce is like knowing that your mom or dad has cancer. It doesn't mean you'll get it too, but you think about it a lot," Martin, a perceptive youngster, told me.

Even if their parents' divorce made sense to them, adolescents may still be bruised by the poor model of marriage they grew up with. They have received one-sided answers from the two sides. And if they don't understand why their parents split up, they may think a lot about it, yet not ask questions. They may look to you, hoping to find answers.

Be smart. Keep your relationship with your grandchildren separate from your relationship with their parents (your adult child and your former in-law). Each generation's problems should stay within the boundary of that system of relationships.

Ask questions that let your grandchildren of divorce talk about their ideas and feelings. Be careful not to prod; just open the door with casual comments. Tell them about the times you moved, changed schools, lost friends, got your first job, and so on. If you have been divorced (or if your parents were), share what you've learned. These real-life stories of courage will help them face changes in their own lives.

Psychologist and seminary professor Archibald Hart, who was twelve years old when his parents divorced, remembers his grandparents' home as an oasis of calm. "As children sense your peace, they are apt to emulate that attitude," he says.[1] But

Dr. Hart cautions that grandparents must themselves be free of resentment in order to offer comforting refuge. And remember, children read your body language even better than words, so beware!

> *Pay particular attention to body language, yours and your grandchildren's. What does their body language tell you about their feelings?*

If your grandchildren are reacting to family changes caused by divorce, your own tolerance will help them to be tolerant also. Mention ways that others, including "exes" you don't necessarily like, are probably struggling too. Appealing to a sense of team spirit can sometimes rally uncooperative adolescents.

Be understanding when your grandchild's schoolwork suffers, if they have trouble establishing close friendships, or if they seem insecure about their sexual identities. The intensity and duration of these personality problems largely depends on reestablishing stability in the family. You can help by

- talking honestly about what is happening in the family;
- reminding them that you will always feel close to them;
- allowing them to express their feelings of fear or anger;
- assuring them that they're loved.

Bringing up sensitive issues is easier when you are doing things together. Pull weeds together in the garden. Get involved in a mutual hobby. Go for a drive—it gives a lot of time to talk, and you don't have to look each other in the eye. Be sure to tell your adolescent grandchild that you're praying for them and everyone in their family every day.

RELATING TO TEEN GRANDCHILDREN

With grandchildren who are teens, you'll go through the same undefined rites of passage that you did with your own children. Be a sounding board as they explore emerging adulthood. Your grandchildren will probably allow you to express your viewpoint more than your own teenagers did. But when your viewpoints differ, remember *your* values are not *their* values until they themselves make that choice.

A family divorce causes some teens to grow up faster than others their age. They carry more responsibility and they're expected to be more independent. They see that their parents aren't perfect people. Their parents are more like peers than like "mom and dad." After all, their parents are single, as they are.

Read James 3:17–18. How can you apply this passage to your grandchildren?

Teenagers of divorce are usually reluctant to accept that either parent is dating (especially the custodial parent). They find it awkward, if not impossible, to picture their mom or dad having a romantic interest in the opposite sex. Your open acceptance of your adult child as an attractive sexual person will help mold your teen grandchild's image of his single parent. Don't pry information from the teen about his parents' dating life, though. And if they offer information, don't overreact. ("Oh? Uh-huh," is a safe retort.) Instead of a comment, you might ask them how *they* feel about the new relationship.

Older teenagers' ideas about sexual mores are likely to differ from yours. A study at Indiana University in 1989 indicates that college-age students from divorced families are a stunning 54 percent more likely to cohabit than are contemporaries whose parents are still married.[2] As you talk about values and sexual issues, make it clear that you're stating your own opinion, not judging others.

A nondefensive attitude about (not necessarily agreement with) your teen grandchild's own life is your best stance. Show that you're interested in learning what life is like for her generation. If you listen well, you may be able to discuss your beliefs about prayerful choices and covenant commitments.

How else can you relate to a teenage grandchild? Lifestyle differences abound! You may listen to the philharmonic; your teenage grandchild probably listens to rap. You get lost in the terminology of computerese, as familiar to them as a cookbook recipe is to you. Be willing to try new things. Make a deal with visiting teens to alternate "music-choice hours"; they'll have the even hours, you the odd. In the same way, create daily menus. Take turns choosing between lamb with basil (your choice), and Hawaiian-topped pizza (their choice).

Teenagers need structure. If you have chores they could do, put them to work. Plan a reward after a few hours of yard work or washing the car. If you're limited by a small condo in the city, shift the emphasis. Visit a shelter for homeless families and take along food you have prepared together. (Call ahead to make arrangements for your visit.)

Read Ephesians 5:15–17.
Are you "careful how you live"? Do you
"make the most of every opportunity"?

When you're watching TV, ask questions during commercials to discover what your grandchildren are thinking. Don't ask questions that have obvious yes or no answers. Instead, ask about their impressions of characters in a drama, or their opinions about a news story. Of course, in your home, you can veto certain TV programs; just be sure to graciously give a logical explanation.

Sharing your views about the environment, politics, hobbies, and intellectual pursuits demonstrates a full and satisfying life to a teenage grandchild. If they see you reading Scripture each day, they're more likely to respect it as a good road map for their own life. And when you pray out loud at the table or bedtime, they'll sense your belief in God's provision.

In the following role-play, how does Darin's grandfather try to keep family solidarity and also listen to the needs of seventeen-year-old Darin? Someone in your group might volunteer to videotape this scene with a teenager. Use the tape as a discussion starter.

Cast: Darin, high-school-age grandson; Darin's paternal grandfather

Scene: Grandpa's backyard. Grandpa (G.P., to Darin) is chopping wood. Darin comes onstage.

Darin: Hi, Grandpa! How's it going?

Grandpa: Well, hello, Darin. I didn't expect you after school today. What's up?

Darin: Oh, nothin' much. I just had a little time before I go on my shift at McDonalds.

Grandpa: What do you think of that job? Would you like to look for something else this summer?

Darin: Probably not, G.P. It's fine for now. Well, uh . . . I was wondering if you and Mimi are going to be going out this Saturday night.

Grandpa: I don't think so. But, then, I don't always know every plan. Why? Got something in mind?

Darin: I was just wondering if I could borrow your car for just that one night. I have a good driving record, you know. There's a big junior class party at school. I really need a car that night!

Grandpa: I sure remember how many times I had to borrow my folks' car. Your dad and stepmother both have cars. What about one of those?

Darin: They've promised me a car for prom night in two weeks. But this date is really important. Debbie—that's my girlfriend—her folks have lots of money. She has a car of her own.

Grandpa: Ummm . . . Have you thought about letting Debbie drive? Or, I tell you what. I'll take you to pick her up for the party. And I'll stay up late to come for you. What do you say?

Darin:	Thanks, G.P., for the offer. But I'd rather have a car. This is our first date and I really want to impress her. Don't you see?
Grandpa:	I guess I don't see yet about your dad and Joyce. Shall I talk with them about this?
Darin:	Oh, no . . . don't do that! I guess you need to know that Joyce has grounded me from driving for one week. Not anything about the car, you understand. I was sort of late coming home last weekend. And, well, that's how it is.
Grandpa:	You find Joyce a lot more strict than your mother, I suspect. Do you think your stepmom would approve of your driving our car if she doesn't want you driving at all right now? I'd like to help you out, Darin, but I might get into trouble with your family.
Darin:	If I left for the party from your house, Joyce wouldn't have to know how I'm going to get there. I could work in exchange for using your car. What d'ya say, G.P.? Could I chop that wood for you?
Grandpa:	I'd sure pay to have those logs split up. But, about the car, I'm sorry I can't make a decision until I've checked things out with your stepmom. We'll see what's possible. Say, would you like to bring Debbie over here sometime? Maybe she could help stack the wood you chop and we'll treat you both to some pizza. You seem to like Debbie a lot. We'd like to get to know her.

How does the grandfather avoid interfering in family discipline? How did he show family fairness? Are Darin and his grandfather close? How do you think Darin will take it if his grandfather's final decision is no, based on what his dad and stepmother say?

It's not easy to keep from making new rules you feel are necessary, or to let the parent enforce rules you feel are unfair. But only if your grandchild's safety or emotional stability is clearly at risk should you step in to defy his parents' position. One book for the mid-generation suggests a "coaching approach." In this plan, the parent is the "head coach," and the grandparents are "assistant coaches." The head coach calls the plays.[3] Notice how Darin's grandfather remained an "assistant coach," giving helpful suggestions from the sidelines. Before calling a "play," he checked with Darin's dad, the "head coach" in this family.

THE GRANDFATHER AS "FATHER FIGURE"

More fathers are now awarded custody, and joint custody is growing in popularity even faster. Still, children of divorce are more apt to lose daily contact with their fathers than with their mothers. A young boy may develop a love-hate relationship with his father in this uncertain scenario. He wants his dad all the time, but he can't have it that way.

While attending the college graduation of Cody's divorced mom in Bakersfield, California, Grandmother Lynn and junior-high-age grandson, Cody, talked to me about the residual hurt and anger in their family. Although Lynn knows where her former son-in-law lives, Cody metaphorically ranted, "My dad is dead. I don't know where he's buried, but he is!" Cody plans to change his name when he's eighteen. He doesn't want his father's name, so strong are his feelings.

Grandfathers can help their grandsons who rebel against their fathers. Through granddads, these male children can find new hope for their ego and for their gender. Author Charles Scull says, "Here is a key to the grandfather's role in a young boy's life: He can reminisce with, love, and enjoy the boy without feeling, as the father does, the need to create a fledgling man who reflects well on himself as masculine standard bearer."[4]

"Our grandkids helped us see the 'big picture' of life," say Claire and Bill Helix, the Arizona couple who have two divorced families with children. Says Claire, "Bill is the only man in the family for our grandsons. And I think he's a better grandparent than he was a parent. He's wiser. He was so young and worked so hard when he was a father. Now, when he plays with the grandkids, I really admire him."

"Claire and I are working together better as grandparents," Bill offers. "I haven't gotten to do as much serious fishing as I had planned, but I bait a lot of little hooks."

Norma and Ed, in Arkansas, ached for their grandsons when they saw other dads and sons playing together in the street. Their grandsons don't have a dad around now. Ed, who says, "I'm not as spry as I used to be," gets out there and plays ball anyway.

DISCIPLINE MATTERS

Disagreement about how to rear children is sure to produce tension unless parental authority is preserved. Babysitting is acceptable; discipline and directing are not. Have children age two and older listen to instructions about expected behavior from their parent while all three generations are present. "Everyone knowing the ground rules keeps me from walking on egg shells," said one grandmother.

When possible, follow the routine younger children are used to. Big rules, like bedtime, should be consistent. Gently and briefly explain the few rules that are nonnegotiable. Children try harder to please when they clearly understand. When your grandchild asks for special permission, say, "Your dad (or mother) and I think . . ." This lets him know that you respect parental authority even when his parent isn't there.

It's best not to have secrets with grandchildren, even seemingly innocent things such as where "forbidden" candy is hidden, or playing unallowed video games. Anything a child is not able to talk about freely with his parent undermines family solidarity.

Angelica, a Native American, was awarded custody of her three-year-old granddaughter after Rosita's mother had been twice divorced. "I wanted to keep Rosita in the family," Angelica said. "Now she's a teenager and when I don't let her have her way, she runs back to her mother. The last time, I told her she couldn't come back to me unless I legally adopt her." This grandmother, who values family bonds, is also learning to set boundaries.

Read Proverbs 25:12. Do you "rebuke" wisely? Instead of saying "no" often, show grandchildren a better way or offer acceptable choices.

Harold and Elise added two preschoolers to their household when their daughter, Abbie, moved home for four months. "We felt so unprepared to handle youngsters again," these grandparents told me as I moved toys off their living room sofa to make a place to sit. "Abbie never spanked them; we thought they *needed* a gentle whop sometimes! I was nervous having them alone for very long," Elise said.

Harold recalls the day Abbie overreacted to differences about discipline and got into a fist fight with her mother. "I had to be the authority in that one. Things were out of control!" Harold exclaimed. Within a week, Abbie and her children moved to a small apartment nearby. "It was a better living arrangement," admits Harold, "but an unfortunate way for it to happen."

TEACHING ETHICS; SHARING FAITH

Ethical issues are easier to talk about when set in fiction, whether from the classic *Aesop's Fables* or William Bennett's popular *Book of Virtues*. When you're reading a story to your grandchildren, ask them to tell you words they don't understand. Later, talk about the meanings. Christian grandparents are especially prone to moralizing. You'll probably be tuned out, unless your grandchildren initiate the questions.

A poll touted as the first national three-generation survey found three things grandparents most commonly did with grandchildren: joke, give money, and watch TV. Only 43 percent said they had attended church with their grandchildren in the previous year.[5] To encourage grandchildren to want to go with you to worship, arrange informal times at your home or a park with other youngsters their age who attend your church.

Mike and Gail, southern-style grandparents, were not yet Christians when they raised their own children. "We're closer to our grandchildren since their mother's divorce," Gail said. "And we see the opportunities to influence their lives for the Lord that we didn't have with our own children."

As with Mike and Gail, you can be significant spiritual catalysts. Here are some ways to share your faith with your grandchildren:

- Read or tell them stories about people in the Bible.
- Tell them stories about how God has blessed your family.
- Share a letter their parent sent home from summer camp long ago.
- Take them to Christian musicals and dramas.
- Give them tapes and videos depicting faith.
- Teach little ones finger-play songs about Jesus.
- Talk about how God guides you; thank him for answers.
- Ask them to notice things God is doing in their lives.[6]

Can you talk about Jesus naturally with your grandchildren? Read 1 Peter 3:15. In what ways do you share your faith?

The Chans recalled that when their young grandchildren came to stay with them, the youngsters turned their faces to the wall when Ruth and Peter said table grace. "But, with patience and understanding, the children were soon making up songs to sing for mealtime prayers," Ruth says. The Chans' difficult year of caring for their daughter and her children was worth it all when their five-year-old grandson said with pride: "When I grow up, I want to tell people about Jesus just the way Pa-pa does."

GRANDPARENTS AS ROLE MODELS

As they grow up, your grandchildren of divorce will relish the happy feeling of being with you more than they'll remember specific things they learned. Affirm things you enjoy about them: "I like the twinkle in your eyes . . . the way you handle the baseball bat . . . and how you take care of your kitty."

Your grandchildren need you to praise their handiwork, music skills, good grades, and athletic achievements. Sometimes, just exclaim your joy in having them as your very own grandkid, a special part of your family. Your pride helps build their confidence and self-esteem—and it costs nothing.

Keep a diary of things you see your grandchildren doing at school, church, their first job, and so on. This memento makes a priceless high school graduation gift. Looking back will be easier when they read your chronicle filled with positive images. Without such documented memories, they may remember the aftermath of divorce only as a negative time in their lives.

Grandparents give a priceless gift, too, when they just listen. "Children [of divorce] need someone with whom to talk, pour out their feelings, admit their fears, and share their dreams. Their friends don't understand or may not care, and mom and dad may get upset or want to argue."[7]

Grandparents who can let go of anger and accusations in the heat of conflict give a good gift to their grandchildren. Chances are the grandchildren did not often see that model in their own home prior to the divorce. From you, they can learn acceptable patterns of confrontation and how to negotiate without misunderstanding.

The creative things you do now with your grandchildren of divorce will influence both them and *their* children. Life must be lived forward, but understood backwards. Grandchildren in a divorce may not feel that life is fair (it isn't!). My author friend, Carolyn Johnson, sums up well the best position for the mid-generation: stand back, stand by, and stand watch.

As you interact with your grandchildren you'll be stretched to try new ideas and you'll keep up with the times. You'll also have ample opportunities to pass on a heritage filled with examples of a living faith. Relating to grandchildren of divorce is a challenge well worth the rewards.

13

BONDING THROUGH FRIENDSHIP, LOVE, AND HOPE

As best you can, you've accepted the reality of your child's divorce and the changes it's made in your family circle. You turned your den back into a bedroom when Bonnie came home for a year. Actually, you got to know her better as a person in her own right during that time. You helped her train for a new job; you cared for her preschooler. A while ago, she moved into her own apartment, and Samantha, just turned six, loves to come to Gammie and Grandpa's house.

Things seem to be going pretty well on the surface. But, underneath, you still long to share more deeply with Bonnie. You want to be a loving parent. You want to have hope. It seems hard to talk with her about life's meaning. You wish your own faith were stronger, then maybe she would want to follow your leading.

PRAY FOR YOURSELF

Pray for yourself—you need it! Pray for wisdom. Pray for peace in your heart and throughout your family. Pray to be understanding, even when your viewpoint is not understood. God appreciates your efforts to be a good parent. He loves you. He accepts you. He answers your prayers in his own way.

Prayer is always the starting point for moving toward God. "Rather than seeing ourselves surrounded by obstacles, we surround our obstacles with prayer. . . . In prayer we set aside our agendas, letting God's priorities become our priorities."[1]

Two of Colette's seven children divorced. During those difficult years, Colette and her husband began a practice of holding hands and praying the Lord's Prayer before going to sleep each night. "We found when we asked God to 'forgive us our trespasses,' we had a clean slate to look forward to the next day," Colette said.

It also helps to find a nonfamily prayer partner who is available to you day or night, someone to whom you can comfortably be accountable. Together, pray for emotional and mental stability; to know the immeasurable love of God. Most of all, pray, "Dear God . . . Your will be done." Then someday, with Lillian, the long-suffering mother of Casey, you can say: "God is using everything that happens in my life to make me a stronger and better person."

Psychologist Archibald Hart talked with me about prayer: "Prayer brings healing; prayer keeps us sane," he said. "Prayer helps us see things God's way." What would Dr. Hart suggest that parents pray for? "Strength to take life's blows with grace; for understanding and patience; and for God to show them how to be loving and forgiving."[2]

In a paraphrase of Philippians 4, Eugene Peterson sums up the value of a prayer-filled life: "I'd say you'll do best by filling your minds and meditating on things true, noble, reputable, authentic, compelling, gracious—the best, not the worst; the beautiful, not the ugly; things to praise, not things to curse."[3]

PRAY FOR YOUR DIVORCED CHILD

Your divorced son or daughter is tackling "emotional tigers" every day—loneliness, sexual frustrations, financial insecurity, an uncertain future, single-parenting responsibilities—all the while trying to keep peace with an ex-spouse. You can intercede! Pray for protection for your adult child whose passions are fragile.

Praying for your adult child can reset hope in her heart. You communicate hope and confidence when you tell her, "I'm praying for you every day." Ask for specific things to pray about. Since Leonor began telling her divorced daughter, Angelita, "God is with you wherever you are," Angelita confides that she now thinks about God and prays to him too.

If you pray with your adult child, don't use prayer as a way to indirectly give advice. Singles told me that simple requests for strength are the most comforting prayers. If you share faith with your son or daughter, periodically ask them to pray for a need *you* have. Sharing concerns affirms interdependence, a goal of mature adult friendship.

Read 1 Thessalonians 5:17–18. When are we to pray? Read James 1:5 and Psalm 32:8. What does God give through prayer? Read Philippians 4:4–7 and Isaiah 30:20–21. What are the results of prayer? Read Romans 8:26. How does the Holy Spirit help us?

Be cautious about giving spiritual counsel to your adult child. Simply say, "I care about you. God loves you and so do I." Rose, the faithfully praying mother in Virginia, is heart-warmed by funny "lifestyle" cards from her single-parent daughter. Below her signature, Molly scribbles, "Thanks, Mom, for praying for me." Vital prayer springs from faith, not from fear. Prayer motivated by fear is self-centered rather than God-centered; it misses the mark. God sees how hard parents try, not just how they seem to fail. Angelica said of her divorced daughters, "I put them in the hands of the Lord. All I can do is pray on it."

Real honest-to-goodness prayer doesn't need to be dressed in archaic expressions. God hears our hearts, not just our words. Neither is prayer "Tinker Bell magic," nor dust to sprinkle or buttons to push, expecting an immediate response.

As evangelist Billy Graham explains, prayer is subject to God's will. "We can't manipulate God nor dictate to Him. He is Sovereign. . . . To say, 'Thy will be done' is not a sigh, but a song because His will is always what is best. . . . We cannot find true peace outside of the will of God."[4]

God honors praying parents. Prayer gets us in tune so we can hear God's harmony. "Pray that you'll have the strength to stick it out over the long haul—not the grim strength of gritting your teeth but the glory-strength God gives . . . strength that endures the unendurable and spills over into joy."[5] Yes, *joy!* That's what happens when Christ displaces worry at the center of your life.

GROW IN FAITH

If you sometimes ask, "Where are you, God? Why don't I feel your presence and comfort?" take heart, it's okay to question God. Although we want answers to our everyday problems, the most important answer is finding God. Only a relationship with him brings hope.

Under pressure of divorce in your family, your faith life is forced into the open and shows its true colors. Your impressions of God may be leftover misconceptions from your childhood rather than a genuine personal faith. You try to be good, kind, loving—and wonder why you still don't "measure up." Spirituality without a personal relationship with God comes up lacking. Through the centuries, those who truly trust God have found him to be the one consistent force in a changing world.

Whenever a man or a woman accepts responsibility for "where I am" (confession) and chooses to make a change (repentance) and reaches out for God's love (conversion), then change begins. "We are all free to change, free to be new. . . . Change is the natural order of things when God is at work among us. We need to go with—to flow with—his stream of life-changing growth."[6] As a midlife parent, expect change. Plan for it. Risk it. God's strength makes it possible.

Meaning in life is best framed within the family. God wants us to be part of his spiritual family, a relationship that comes not through a bloodline, but through the line of faith. When we know God as the Ultimate Parent, we appreciate the bonds that weave through generations. Earthly parenting parallels our Heavenly Father's nature. In faith, we're part of his forever family, from whom we draw courage to survive. As one mother summed up: "Knowing that the Almighty was there every step of the way was my hope."

The Holy Spirit is the gift of God's presence with us, guiding us along the best pathway for our lives (see Psalm 32:8). Jesus explained this spiritual mystery: "The wind blows wherever it pleases. You hear its sound, but you cannot tell where it comes from or where it is going. So it is with everyone born of the Spirit" (John 3:8). The Holy Spirit enables us to keep going when our own engine slows to idle.

---

*Read 2 Timothy 3:16. How are we to use
Scripture? After reading God's Word,
what are we to do? Read James 1:22–25.*

The Bible—the sourcebook for life—helps us deal with life's problems in creative ways. The central theme of the Bible is reconciliation. It shows that healing love is available to the most acutely hurting families. Lydia sums up her experience following the divorce of her daughter: "There are no guarantees that life will not hurt. We are fragile, flawed human beings. The best solace and advice I found was the Word of God."

Writer Jane Johnson Struck talks about how the message of the Bible keeps her thinking positively: "I've found it comforting to memorize Scriptures that remind me of God's constant care and availability. When I allow ... verses to settle deep within my heart . . . I have the ammunition I need to help keep my negative thoughts at bay."[7]

Dora and Kurt's faith grew during the frustrating months of having their ill-tempered son, Brad, and his teenage son living with them. "God doesn't bring things into our lives without a way to grow through them," Dora confides. "It's not easy to say 'teach me, Lord,' but I'm glad I did." Kurt grew too. He talked about learning to pray even while talking. "And when I listened to God, I could listen to Brad as well," Kurt says.

Read 1 Peter 1:21: In whom is your faith and hope? If you have doubts about God, where are you seeking answers? In 1 Peter 3:15, what are Christians prepared to do?

My friend Barbra Minar, who has endured many trials as a parent, talks about her faith: "Giving God my mind . . . is like having my most beloved friend with me no matter what I'm doing. Loving me, guiding me, celebrating, laughing, and crying with me—this is what the deep journey is about."[8]

"Life is always a miracle. And miracles are intended to happen within, through and around you and me!" says pastor and grandfather Jack Hayford.[9] Miracles happen as parents depend on God. Parents of divorced adults can be a stable linchpin to anchor God's grace and love. "Every family heritage of faithfulness must begin with someone. . . . At this very moment, it could begin with you."[10] In faith we find God—we also find ourselves.

BE A WITNESS

Christian parents long for their offspring to share their belief. Faith is bonding glue. As you seek ways to share your faith, value your adult child more than you value an issue. The best way to convey theology is through relationship. I hope the ideas in this book have helped you develop a stronger and closer relationship with God the Father, and with your divorced child. Faith is taught more than it is caught!

Sometimes parents and adult children misunderstand each other's motives. For example, consider the differences in these interchanges:

Parent: "We're going to nine o'clock church tomorrow. Would you like to come with us?"

Adult son: "No, I've got to fix my car."

Parent: "It seems to me you could spend just one hour a week in church."

The parent thinks the son is finding excuses. The son's real reason for declining is that he feels as if he doesn't know anyone at his parents' church. The son thinks his parents want to tell him what to do. The parents' real reason for inviting him is their concern for their son's salvation.

You may be discouraged if your adult child is more interested in sports and "surfing the Net" than spiritual things. Be prayerful and patient about matters of faith. Deep spiritual growth comes from within, and in its own time. Baby boomers, many now in their forties, see life as a spiritual journey rather than a commitment to a fixed doctrine. And Generation X, the twenty-something generation, is concerned with how people live, not what they believe. Spirituality doesn't come from understanding a ritual, but from experiencing it. They see themselves as spiritual seekers who gravitate to "journal theology" —a metaphor for personal growth. Just because they don't relate to traditional worship doesn't necessarily mean your adult children have turned from God. They're looking for an interactive faith.

Norma and Ed in the Ozarks talk about the "dry time" when their daughter, Amanda, had avoided the church. But after a divorce, this single mom began to depend on the Lord. Even when she had only one good dress to wear, Amanda and her children began to regularly go to church.

Bernice, an inner-city African-American, is still praying for that turnaround in her divorced daughter's life. "I brought

Athelda up in the church, but she feels like life has dealt her a bad hand and has turned from God," Bernice says with a sigh. "I can pray for her but I can't manipulate her."

Sometimes the choices our grown children make are just different from ours, not necessarily wrong. Martie, Joleen and Al's daughter, considered Alanon a "substitute church" for awhile. Gradually, her faith began to grow as she saw God working through her difficulties.

Our adult children were in our care during their growing years, but they belong to God forever. Ultimately, your adult child needs to cast off your authority as parent and transfer that allegiance to God. As Rev. Campbell's daughter, Shana, confesses, "For me divorce was quite a wringer! I had to see that without God in my life I had nothing of value." Shana credits both God and her parents: "My family was there for me, helping me to be a good mother to Justin. And they did more to bring me closer to God than anyone [else] in my life."

Like Shana's parents, your goal is to help your adult children trust God for their provision—not you. Here's how, says author Bob Pedrick, in his book *The Confident Parent:* "Pray much, preach little; stroke often, strike seldom. Listen much, let go. . . . The lasting effect of good parenting is as immortal as the love that motivates it."[11]

Do your adult children and their children know how and why you came to believe? Write out your beliefs for your grandchildren's baby books. Plan a "heritage night dinner" (maybe on your birthday) with the announced purpose of telling your story of faith. During dessert, share meaningful memorabilia and personal experiences.

You may occasionally want to continue extending invitations to join you in worship: "Dad and I would enjoy having you join us this Sunday for ten o'clock worship and brunch afterward." But even if you wrap the package of faith attractively, your adult children must unwrap it for themselves. Until then, they'll resent manipulations.

Church programs alone will never meet your adult child's needs like Jesus does. Only his love can cover hurts and frustrations with the same gentleness parents used when tucking their children into bed at night when they were young. You cannot "save" your children; only a Savior can. Your life is your witness. As a Christian, daily live out your faith so it is both believable and believed.

Could you send a letter about these things to your divorced son or daughter? Plan to invite your grown child to lunch and tell him or her how much he or she means to you. Risk loving!

Either in a group or with a friend, try the following exercise. Two people pair up to simulate a parent and a divorced child. When it is your turn to play the "parent," take time to collect your thoughts about your adult child. Tell him why you appreciate him. If needed, ask for specific forgiveness. Express your desire for closeness. Suggest a fun thing you could do together soon. Tell your child what your faith means to you, that you are praying for him, and why you have hope for him. Reverse roles and repeat. If you're journaling, write down your thoughts.

HOPE—LIVE IT, SHARE IT

Proverbs 13:12 in the *Good News Bible* reads: "When hope is crushed, the heart is crushed, but a wish come true fills you with joy." Why is hope so critical? "God wants His message of encouragement to get through to us. Otherwise our minds become deafened by the roar of circumstances and our hearts close up to hope."[12] Penance is tied to the past. Courage to restore relationships belongs to the future. We wish we could see ahead, but we can't. Hope makes the difference.

With God as the "wind beneath our wings," we see the positives more easily, and hope more assuredly. Hope is not a dream or wishful thinking. God's daily promise is a reality—his omnipresence.

The lifelines connecting our past, present, and future are kept taut by hope—hope that springs from an enduring faith. Share it. Live it. Write it on the doorpost of your heart! Hope looks to the future—without hope, something inside all of us dies.

Praise God for his daily help in parenting your adult child. Prayerfully read Psalm 145.

Wise parents learn to pave the path with pebbles of hope. Hope keeps us on an even keel over the long haul. The passage of time smooths the rough road we've traveled with our adult child through the ruts of divorce. Jesus was there then, and he's present now. Someday, as we look back, the journey will take on new meaning.

Theologian Lewis Smedes reminds us that hope is not a Christian invention; it's common to our humanity.

> Hope is the spirit's vital breath. It is to the spirit what oxygen is to the lungs. Without it, we die inside. With it, we live. Hope sets its heart on the possibility of good.... Hope is also the power that enables us to wait when there's nothing we can do to make the possible become reality. Waiting often takes more creative courage than working.[13]

When our divorced child is despondent, can we still hope? "Christian hope ... is no longer a passion for the possible. It becomes a passion for the *promise*," answers Smedes. And what does God promise? "He promises he will sustain us as we walk into a tomorrow we can imagine but cannot control." We cannot hold God to making our hopes and dreams for our divorced children come true. Yet, "he promises to be with us, whether our hopes come true or not ... he is there to hold us, pick us up, and lead us into the future,"[14] Smedes says.

CHOOSE TO LOVE

God's plan for our relationship to our adult children is summarized in one word—love. We loved them the way they were when they came into the world, and we love them now because we see, through prayer, the possibilities for their future. Loving divorced children involves us in pain. In fact, love and suffering often seem to go together. We love, but we cannot demand its return. Only through grasping God's love can we love the unlovable.

Any loss of connection to our grown child—anger, fear, and other parenting frustrations—reflects our inadequate love. Love begins with a deliberate decision to be kind. Sometimes we have to put aside our first impulse and *will* to love. The gift of love is not based on what our adult child does or doesn't do; rather, it's based on our desire for relationship. Shana's father, the convivial Rev. Campbell, says "Make the message of love loud and clear . . . Parents should never leave grown children in doubt about their love."

Love is an imperative! It's how we are made. "Love is a healing force. I believe that firmly!" says Irma, describing the ripples of pain after her son's divorce. This mom had discovered that loving is for our *own* good. The more we give love, the more we have left over.

In a *Focus on the Family* newsletter, James Dobson says that "even in those cases where the single-parent situation resulted from sin, we must reach out in love. . . . God loves the sinner . . . [God] asks those who know Him to be part of the healing process."[15] Healing love believes the best and never gives up. Deep within, we are disarmed with God's love.

Read 1 Corinthians 13 out loud.
Read 1 John 4:7–12. What is true love?

Sherry, a devoted mother, steadfastly prayed for her daughter Liz as she unwisely married, lived through four stormy years, and divorced. Although Sherry and Liz have a cordial relationship, they are not emotionally close. Sherry talks about searching for an appropriate card for Liz's twenty-fifth birthday. "Most of the cards seemed too gushy," Sherry says. "I couldn't honestly say that Liz had been the 'apple of my eye' or was 'always the perfect daughter.'"

About ready to give up, Sherry reached higher on the rack for a card with a single pink rose embossed on the cover. "To My Daughter," it read. Inside was a simple message: "Although many good wishes will come your way today, may this one speak to your heart—I love you."

"After all," Sherry says with a sigh, "when Liz was little I didn't love her only when she was good. I loved her *regardless*. I'm trying to recapture that attitude." Sherry has found that parental love is a matter of the heart. It is knowing the person your child *can be* but *isn't yet*.

Parents and adult children depend on love to link the generations. Christian love binds up broken circles. The oft-quoted message of love in 1 Corinthians 13 guides us: "Until that completeness, we have three things to do.... Trust steadily in God, hope unswervingly, love extravagantly. And the best of the three is love."[16]

"Love doesn't sit back and snooze," says popular author and Christian radio personality Chuck Swindoll. Love "is not apathetic. It is ready and willing. It is neither passive nor indifferent. It refuses to yawn its way through life. Authentic love is demonstrative, not sterile and dull."[17]

Parents are special people. God, the source of unconditional love, will give you the grace to love your grown children through *anything*—even in the darkest days after their divorce. When your parenting days are over (at life's end), three things will matter most: Who loved you; whom you loved; and what you did for God.

With hope and love, peace begins to settle in your soul. The suffocating sense of panic *(What will I say to my friends?)* you first felt about the divorce dies down. The darkness of despair lifts and hope begins to shine through. Today is better than yesterday; you look forward to tomorrow. You are free to think of other things again.

Colors are more vibrant, music more satisfying, the taste of food more delightful. You laugh more easily. "This is the day that the Lord has made, let us rejoice and be glad!" you say—and really mean it. You've stopped trying so hard to understand life; instead, you are going to live it! You plan for your future. You have a new interest in helping others—in serving.

Ah, that's the key! Real life and real love are found in serving. And parents *do* serve! From birth through growing years to maturity. Parents give to their children in many ways. "It's an unfolding adventure that can only be known through being committed to parenthood—all the way home!"[18]

Whether you've just heard about your child's divorce or whether you're helping her sort through the flood of changes, meet each day with hope. Believe that your broken or mending family can rebond with God's love. As you hope in him, he will surprise you with unending help and confidence.

RESOURCES

ALCOHOL AND SUBSTANCE ABUSE

Alcoholics Anonymous. For education, counseling, and recovery of alcoholics and their families. Consult the white pages of your phone directory for local listing.

Clearing House for Alcohol and Drug Dependency. Write: P.O. Box 2345, Rockville, MD 20852. Call: 1–800–729–6886.

National Clearing House for Alcohol Information. Publishes free booklets. This department of Health and Human Services maintains an electronic "home page" at www.health.org. Call: (301) 468–2600.

CONCILIATION AND MEDIATION

Academy of Family Mediators (AFM). Provides information on trained and experienced family mediators throughout the United States, Canada, and sixteen other countries. Write: 4 Militia Drive, Lexington, MA 02173. Call: (617) 674–2663.

SPIDER. Helps locate local professionals for legal dispute resolution. Call: (202) 783–7277.

DIVORCE RECOVERY

Fresh Start. Hosts seminars throughout the United States. Publishes resources for divorce recovery. Write: 63 Chestnut Road, Paoli, PA 19301. Call: 1–800–882–2799.

Single Ministries Resources. Provides a listing of ministries on divorce recovery and single parenting. Write: P.O. Box 36670, Colorado Springs, CO 80936. Call: (719) 533–3041.

FAMILY ISSUES

Christian Family Movement. An ecumenical network of parish and neighborhood families, including single parents. Directed in the United States by Roman Catholic lay leaders. Ministry programs include, "The Hope and Promise for a New Tomorrow," for divorce adjustment. Newsletter: *ACT.* Write: P.O. Box 272, Ames, IA 50010. Call: (515) 232–7432.

Family Service America, Inc. International association of agencies (both sectarian and nonsectarian); most offer programs on coping with divorce and divorce mediation. Maintains the Severson National Information Center, including a research library (fees), publications catalog (free). Write: 11700 West Lake Park Drive, Milwaukee, WI 53224. Call: (414) 359–1040 for the Severson Center.

National Council on Child Abuse and Family Violence. Provides referrals twenty-four hours a day. Call: 1–800–222–2000.

Stepfamily Association of America. Provides education and support for adults and children of divorce; listing of professional counselors. Publishes books about divorce and step-parenting. Newsletter: *Stepfamilies.* Write: 215 Centennial Mall South, Suite 212, Lincoln, NE 68508. Call: 1–800–735–0329.

Tough Love. An international organization that encourages parents and grandparents to work together to maintain positive behavior changes in their family members (ages 8–40) during crisis situations. Write: P.O. Box 1069, Doylestown, PA 18901. Call: 1–800–333–1069.

GRANDPARENTING

American Association of Retired Persons (AARP). Grandparent information center provides information and referral resources to grandparents raising grandchildren. Call: (202) 434–2296.

Grandparents Rights Organization. Legal information and political advocacy for grandparents who are denied kinship rights by parents, or by courts. Write: 555 S. Woodward, Suite 600, Birmingham, MI 48009. Call: (810) 646–7191.

ROCKING, Inc. An acronym for Raising Our Children's Kids: An Intergenerational Network of Grandparenting, Inc. ROCKING offers practical advice to grandparent caregivers who are looking for resources to keep their families intact. Write: P.O. Box 96, Niles, MI 49120. Call: (616) 683–2058.

LEGAL AFFAIRS

Legal Aid Referral Services. Referrals for gratis legal assistance. Call: (816) 795–1555.

National Lawyer Referral Network. Refers callers to a local member of the Christian Legal Society. Call: 1–800–823–9791.

MENTAL HEALTH

Minirth Meier Clinic. Sponsors "New Life" seminars, cassette tapes, and a daily radio show. Call for *Solutions newsletter:* 1–800–676–4673. For clinic locations, call: 1–800–229–3000.

RAPHA. Provides clinical assessment and referrals to mental health resources throughout the United States and Hawaii. Call: 1–800–383–4673 (HOPE).

PREGNANCY

Care Net. Christian pregnancy centers located across the United States. For nearest location, call: (703) 478–5661.

SINGLES

Network of Single Adult Leaders. Equips single adult ministry leaders by providing training, tools, and the encouragement necessary to develop local ministries. Write: NSL, P.O. Box 1600, Grand Rapids, MI 49501. Call: (616) 956–9377.

Single Parents Family Resources. Write: P.O. Box 427, Ballwin, MO 63022. Call: (314) 230–6500.

THERAPY, COUNSELING, AND SELF-HELP GROUPS

American Association for Marriage and Family Therapy. Provides a list of clinical members by zip code area. Brochure: *A Consumer's Guide to Marriage and Family Therapy.* 1100

Seventeenth St., NW, The Tenth Floor, Washington, DC 20036.
Call: 1–800–374-AMFT.

American Self-Help Clearinghouse. Provides referrals to a self- help
group that matches your need. Publishes *The Self-Help Source-book* with contacts for more than 700 national and model self-
help peer groups. St. Clares-Riverside Medical Center, Denville,
NJ 97834. Call: (201) 625–7101. Also maintains a "Self-Help Support" section in the Health and Fitness Forum "go GoodHealth"
on CompuServe.

NOTES

Chapter 1: Hearing the News—and Surviving!

1. In a study of thirty-six grandparents who had experienced the divorce of a child, 40 percent indicated that they were totally surprised by the course of events. *The Gerontology*, 24:1, 1949, 41.

2. James C. Dobson, *Focus on the Family*, September 1995, 2.

3. Michael Mask, Julie L. Mask, Jeanne Hensley, Steven L. Craig, *Family Secrets* (Nashville: Nelson, 1995), 12–13.

4. Walter Wangerin Jr., *Mourning into Dancing* (Grand Rapids: Zondervan, 1992), 97.

5. Dolly Patterson, "Redeeming Failure," unpublished.

6. James Dobson, *When God Doesn't Make Sense* (Wheaton, IL: Tyndale House, 1993), 250.

7. Linda Weber, *Mom, You're Incredible* (Colorado Springs: Focus on the Family, 1994), 118.

8. Barbra Minar, *Unrealistic Expectations* (Wheaton, IL: Victor, 1990), 13.

9. Jan and David Stoop, *Saying Goodbye to Disappointments* (Nashville: Nelson, 1993), 105.

10. Dobson, *When God Doesn't Make Sense*, 47.

11. Neil Clark Warren, *Make Anger Your Ally* (Garden City: Doubleday, 1983), 210.

12. Linda Raney Wright, *Raising Children* (Wheaton, IL: Tyndale House, 1975), page unknown.

13. John Wimber, "Spirit Song," Anaheim, CA: Mercy Publishing. Excerpt used with permission.

Chapter 2: Growing Through the Pain

1. James C. Dobson, *Parenting Isn't for Cowards* (Dallas: Word, 1987), 16.

2. John White, *Parents in Pain* (Downers Grove, IL: InterVarsity Press, 1979), 220.

3. Larry V. Stockman and Cynthia S. Graves, *Adult Children Who Won't Grow Up* (Chicago: Contemporary, 1989), 57.

4. Barbra Minar, from the brochure "Parents in Crisis: Parents in Pain," 2854 Quail Valley Road, Solvang, CA 93463, 1989.

5. Shauna L. Smith, *Making Peace With Your Adult Children* (New York: Plenum, 1991), 343.

6. Chuck Swindoll, *The Strong Family* (Portland, OR: Multnomah Press, 1991), 218.

7. Barbara Johnson, seminar speaker at the Evangelical Press Association annual convention, Anaheim, CA, May 9, 1994.

8. Ruth Senter, *Beyond Safe Places and Easy Answers* (Nashville: Nelson, 1987), 186.

9. Charlene Ann Baumbich, *How to Eat Humble Pie & Not Get Indigestion* (Downers Grove, IL: InterVarsity Press, 1993), 160–63.

10. Randy and Nanci Alcorn, *Women Under Stress* (Portland, OR: Multnomah Press, 1986), 122.

11. Terry Lackey, "Adult Children Can Conquer Cyclical Family Dysfunctions," *Baptist Press* (March 24, 1994). Review of message by Kay Moore at the National Conference of Recovery and Spiritual Awakening in Euless, Texas.

Chapter 3: Listening to Your Divorced Son or Daughter
1. Written survey of one hundred divorced adults by author, 1995.
2. Walter Wangerin Jr., *Mourning into Dancing*, 176.
3. Telephone interview with Jim Conway, 1990.

Chapter 4: Staying in Touch with Your Single-Again Child
1. Sharon G. Marshall, *When a Friend Gets a Divorce* (Grand Rapids: Baker, 1990), 53.
2. Victoria Secunda, *Reframing the Father-Daughter Relationship* (New York: Delacorte, 1992), 380.
3. H. Norman Wright, *Always Daddy's Girl* (Ventura, CA: Regal, 1989), composite of chapters.
4. Charles S. Scull, *Fathers, Sons, and Daughters* (Los Angeles: Jeremy P. Tarcher, 1992), 201.
5. Evelyn S. Bassoff, *Between Mothers and Sons* (New York: Dutton, Penguin Group, 1994), 3.
6. Ibid., 211.
7. Ibid.

Chapter 5: Coping with Singles Back Home Again
1. Stephen Bly, *Just Because They've Left Doesn't Mean They're Gone* (Colorado Springs: Focus on the Family, 1993), 109.
2. Adapted from Jerry and Mary White, *When Your Kids Aren't Kids Anymore* (Colorado Springs: NavPress, 1989), 115–20.
3. Telephone interview with Jim Conway, 1990.
4. Tim Stafford, CIN cyber-chat online, August 29, 1995.

Chapter 6: Dealing with Sex, Substance Abuse, and Money

1. Telephone conversation with George Gallup Jr., Chairman, The George H. Gallup International Institute, Princeton, N.J., September 30, 1996.

2. John White, *Parents in Pain*, 156.

3. Tim Stafford, *Sexual Chaos* (Downers Grove, IL: InterVarsity Press, 1993), 123–24.

4. Ibid., 139.

5. Arthur Maslow and Moira Duggan, *Family Connections* (New York: Doubleday, 1982), 137.

6. Henry Cloud and John Townsend, *Boundaries* (Grand Rapids: Zondervan, 1992), 29.

7. Ibid., 222–24.

8. David Veerman, *Parenting Passages* (Wheaton, IL.: Tyndale House, 1994), 260.

9. Shirley Cook, *Grown-up Kids* (Denver: Accent, 1987), 119.

Chapter 7: Adapting to New Family Circles

1. *Current Thoughts & Trends* (April 1995): 10. Citing a paragraph from M. McManus, *Marriage Savers*, 1993.

2. "Current Population Reports," Series P–60, #174, U.S. Dept. of Commerce, Burdeau of the Census (August 1991).

3. "Fast Facts," *Current Thoughts and Trends* (November 1994): 13.

4. *The World Almanac and Book of Facts 1995* (New York: Funk & Wagnalls Corp., 1995). (Between the twelve-month period ending March 1993 and the twelve-month period ending March 1994, the divorce rate declined from 4.7 to 4.6 per 1000.)

5. Arthur Maslow and Moira Duggan, *Family Connections*, 9.

6. Roy W. Fairchild, *Christians in Families* (Richmond, VA.: CLC Press, 1964), 12.

7. Edward W. Beal and Gloria Hockman, *Adult Children of Divorce* (New York: Delacorte, 1991), 25.

8. Ibid., 9.

9. Edith Schaeffer, *What Is a Family?* (London: Hodder and Stoughton, 1975), 30.

Chapter 8: Encouraging the Healing Process

1. Jerry and Mary White, *When Your Kids Aren't Kids Anymore*, 170.

2. Henry Cloud and John Townsend, *Boundaries*, 131.

3. Family Ties, Individual Software, Inc., Pleasanton, CA 94588. Phone 1–800–331–3313.

4. David Augsburger, *Caring Enough to Confront* (Ventura, CA: Regal, 1976), 87.

5. Tim Stafford, electronic interview, August 29, 1995.

6. Archibald Hart, personal interview, Fuller Seminary, December 1988.

7. Lewis Smedes, *Forgive and Forget: Healing the Hurts We Don't Deserve* (San Francisco: HarperCollins, 1991), 141.

8. Gordon MacDonald, "How to Express Forgiveness," *Christian Herald* (March/April, 1991), page unknown.

9. David Stoop and James Masteller, *Forgiving Our Parents, Forgiving Ourselves* (Ann Arbor, MI: Servant, 1991), 179.

10. Michele Halseide, "Do You Keep Score?" *Today's Christian Woman* (November/December 1991), 74.

11. David S. Freeman, *Multigenerational Family Therapy* (New York: Haworth Press, 1992), 20.

12. Shauna L. Smith, *Making Peace with Your Adult Children*, 149–50.

13. Edwin L. Klingelhofer, *Coping With Your Grown Children* (Clifton, NJ: Humana Press, 1989), 8.

14. Maslow and Duggan, *Family Connections*, 184.

15. Henry Cloud, *Changes That Heal* (Grand Rapids, Zondervan, 1992), 57.

Chapter 9: Managing Anger and Building Trust

1. Paula J. Caplan, *Don't Blame Mother: Mending the Mother-Daughter Relationship* (New York: Harper & Row, 1989), 138.

2. Neil Warren, *Make Anger Your Ally*, 137–38.

3. Alice and Robert Fryling, *A Handbook for Parents* (Downer's Grove, IL: InterVarsity Press, 1991), 106.

4. David Augsburger, *Caring Enough to Confront*, 41.

5. Ibid., 52.

6. Eugene Peterson, *The Message* (Colorado Springs: NavPress, 1993), 480.

7. Warren, *Make Anger Your Ally*, 15–16.

8. Shauna L. Smith, *Making Peace with Your Adult Children*, 172.

9. Roger Fisher and William Ury with Bruce Patton, editor, *Getting to Yes* (Boston: Houghton Mifflin, 1991), 11–13.

10. Shirley Campbell, representative for the American Arbitration Association, personal interview, Sonora, CA, May 1995.

11. Augsburger, *Caring Enough to Confront*, 43.

12. Ibid., 69.

13. Jean Davies Okimoto and Phyllis Jackson Stegall, *Boomerang Kids* (Boston: Little, Brown & Co., 1987), 50.

14. Augsburger, *Caring Enough to Confront*, 81.

15. Ibid., 13.

Chapter 10: Polishing the Friendship Between Parent and Adult Child

1. A. M. Gandin, "After the Divorce: Familial Factors That Predict Well-being for Older and Younger Persons," *Journal of Divorce and Remarriage* (1991): 175.

2. David Augsburger, *Caring Enough to Confront*, 83.

3. Life Stories (game), (Pomona, CA:, Talicor, Inc.), 1–800–433–GAME.

4. William Glasser, *Reality Therapy* (New York: Harper & Row, 1965), 15.

5. Eldon and Pauline Trueblood, *The Recovery of Family Life* (New York: Harper & Brothers, 1953), 119.

6. James Dobson, *Parenting Isn't for Cowards*, 209–11.

7. Larry V. Stockman and Cynthia S. Graves, *Adult Children Who Won't Grow Up*, 22.

8. Chuck Swindoll, *Growing Strong in the Seasons of Life* (Portland, OR: Multnomah Press, 1983), 350.

9. Arthur Maslow and Moira Duggan, *Family Connections*, 11.

10. Tim Kimmel, *Powerful Personalities* (Colorado Springs: Focus on the Family, 1993), 179.

Chapter 11: Linking the Family Through Grandparenting

1. Lawrence Kutner, "Parent & Child," *New York Times* (April 7, 1994), C–12.

2. Adapted from Arthur Kornhaber and Kenneth L. Woodward, *Grandparents/Grandchildren: The Vital Connection* (Garden City, NY: Anchor Press/Doubleday, 1981), 184.

3. Ibid.

4. Marjorie Lee Chandler, "When Your Child Divorces," *Today's Christian Woman* (May/June 1992), 44.

5. Kornhaber and Woodward, group II of art inserts.

6. William E. Pannell, telephone interview, September 26, 1996.

7. Andrew J. Cherlin and Frank F. Furstenberg Jr., *The New American Grandparent* (New York: Basic Books, 1986), 187.

8. Arthur Maslow and Moira Duggan, *Family Connections*, 206.

Chapter 12: Relating to Grandchildren of Divorce

1. Interview with Archibald Hart, Fuller Seminary, December 1988.

2. Edward W. Beal and Gloria Hockman, *Adult Children of Divorce*, 29.

3. Jean Davies Okimoto and Phyllis Jackson Stegall, *Boomerang Kids*, 112–16.

4. Charles S. Scull, *Fathers, Sons, and Daughters*, 201.

5. Andrew J. Cherlin and Frank F. Furstenberg Jr., *The New American Grandparent*, 74.

6. Adapted from Jerry and Mary White, *When Your Kids Aren't Kids Anymore*, 137.

7. David Veerman, *Parenting Passages*, 309.

Chapter 13: Bonding Through Friendship, Love, and Hope

1. John F. Westfall, *Coloring Outside the Lines* (San Francisco: Harper, 1991), 158–59.

2. Personal interview with Archibald Hart at Fuller Seminary, December 1988.

3. Eugene Peterson, *The Message*, 421.

4. William Griffin and Ruth Graham Dienert, compilers, *The Faithful Christian: An Anthology of Billy Graham* (New York: McCracken, 1994), 143–44.

5. Peterson, *The Message*, 421.

6. David Augsburger, *Caring Enough to Confront*, 164.

7. Jane Johnson Struck, "Are You a Negaholic?" *Today's Christian Woman* (Nov./Dec., 1991), 92.

8. Barbra Minar, *Unrealistic Expectations*, 164.

9. Jack Hayford, *The Mary Miracle* (Ventura, CA: Regal, 1994), 18–21.

10. Gigi Tchividjian-Graham, *Passing It On* (New York: McCracken, 1993), 93.

11. Bob Pedrick, *The Confident Parent* (Elgin, IL: David C. Cook, 1979), n.p.

12. Hayford, *The Mary Miracle*, 112.

13. Lewis B. Smedes, "Hope, the Power, the Pain and the Passion," *Fuller Focus* (Spring 1995): 10–11.

14. Ibid., 11.

15. James Dobson, *Focus on the Family* newsletter (November 1994): 22.

16. Peterson, *The Message*, 360.

17. Charles Swindoll, *Dropping Your Guard* (New York: Guideposts, 1983), 120–23.

18. Minar, *Unrealistic Expectations*, 38.

ABOUT THE AUTHOR

Marjorie Lee "ML" Chandler, author of nearly two hundred articles, mostly about family issues, gives us her first book. Marjorie Lee contributed to David C. Cook's 1995 anthology, *Christian Parenting Answers.* A former speech and language therapist, she enjoys hiking mountains, reading novels, and seeing plays. Marjorie Lee and her author-husband, Russell, live in central California. They parent a blended family of six grown children and a bevy of grandchildren.

The text of
After Your Child Divorces
was typeset in 11-point ITC Century Book,
a typeface designed by Tony Stan, 1975. Based on
Century Schoolbook by Morris Fuller Benton, 1915.
Composition done by Zondervan Publishing
House Production Department. The
interior was designed by Sue
Vandenberg Koppenol.